Nelson Thornes Primary

ICT

TEACHER'S BOOK

Reception ▶ P 1

Sally Palmer and Roy Jarratt

Series consultant: Tristram Shepard

Published in 2002 by:
Nelson Thornes Ltd
Delta Place
27 Bath Road
CHELTENHAM
GL53 7TH
United Kingdom

02 03 04 05 06 \ 10 9 8 7 6 5 4 3 2 1

A catalogue record for this book is available from the British Library.

ISBN 0 7487 4250 6

Illustrations by Art Construction and Peter Shaw

Page make-up by AMR Ltd

Printed and bound in Great Britain by Antony Rowe

Contents

Introduction

ICT has taken on an increased importance within the curriculum over the past five years. The technology itself has developed rapidly – schools now have computers with CD-ROM drives, sound and video capability and e-mail access as a matter of course. Teachers have taken part in LEA initiatives to increase their own skills and familiarity with computers.

Current initiatives and support

- Skills which the children need to learn are listed clearly in QCA documentation.

- NGFL provides increasing support for teachers and a wide range of resources for the children.

- NOF funding, managed by the TTA, is now available to teachers to enable them to increase their knowledge of planning in terms of targets and teaching objectives. The project also helps teachers to integrate ICT into their literacy and numeracy programmes.

- The revised Programme of Study for ICT, in place from January 2000, shows clearly in its emphasis on presentation and sharing of information, the focus of ICT in the classroom of the future.

How does *Nelson Thornes Primary ICT* help teachers to meet the demands of these new initiatives?

The course provides you with a complete package of materials which enable you to:

- develop your own skills in using the computer

- teach in a confident and targeted way

- plan and assess against defined targets, linked to the Programme of Study

- differentiate the work according to the needs of your class

- teach the children to assess their own work and jointly set targets for development

The course is structured in such a way that teachers know exactly what computer skills to teach each week. It also shows how these fit in with both the Foundation Stage/P1 Curriculum Guidance, particularly in English, mathematics and science. Pupil Work Cards enable teachers to prepare thoroughly for the computer skills they will need to have themselves in order to be confident that the right software and resources are ready each week. The task for the children is clearly given on page one of the Work Card, together with the children's targets for learning for that week. The major advantage of using *Nelson Thornes Primary ICT* is that teachers will see clearly that the planning, teaching and assessment of each unit covers the Foundation Stage/P1 Curriculum Guidance, and also allows them to plan targets into other subjects of the curriculum. Skills given in each lesson are always set into the context of other subjects, making the computer a useful learning tool for knowledge and understanding of the world, for example, as a means of presenting information.

How to use *Nelson Thornes Primary ICT*

Each lesson, planned to take one hour of continuous teaching or to be spread over one week, contains the following items:

- notes for preparation of materials

- a lesson plan

- a large format Flipover Book and Key Questions sheet to introduce the lesson's targets

- pupil Resource Sheets

- a Work Card with computer task

- an extension task for the more able

- an assessment pro forma for the teacher

- a pupil Target Sheet

- additional data files on CD-ROM

- Teacher support files on CD-ROM and in the Teacher's Book

Teachers have a clear pathway from the initial preparation of materials through to the assessment of the learning outcomes for the week.

Further details of each component are outlined below.

Teacher's Book

The Teacher's Book has been designed as a working document which supports the specialist and non-specialist alike in their preparation of each lesson.

Each double page spread contains the necessary information to enable teachers to plan, teach and assess the children's work against a clear, focused target for the week.

Learning intentions are given first, followed by a list of each component you will need for that week to make preparation quicker. A list of new or key vocabulary is given, and supplied in the Resource File as flashcards for you to place around the room for that week.

There follows a step-by-step lesson plan, always given in the same format – introduction using the Flipover Book and Key Questions; whole class discussion of shared work; paired or individual work at the computer and a plenary discussion and sharing of completed work. The lesson plan also contains a series of watchpoints – possible areas where the children may make errors and what you can do about this. The final element of the lesson plan shows you how you may assess the learning which has taken place and record it in your assessment file. At the end of each unit of six weeks, those individual assessments build into an assessment of competence in one or more strands of aspects of the ICT learning within the Foundation Stage/P1.

Organisation of the Unit 4 role play mini-units

Each role-play consists of a whole class introduction at the start of the unit in which the scenario is set, the children's existing knowledge is discussed and explored, and plans are made to create and collect the necessary resources. At the end of each role-play a plenary session is suggested, to draw the role-play to a conclusion and to discuss and consolidate the children's learning.

The activities described within each unit are adult-led, that is they are planned and supported by an adult in either a teaching role or as a play partner to develop children's skills in the use of technology to support their play. For example, an adult helper might be used to guide children on how to use a video recorder to video a news programme in the Television Studio role-play.

The activities are also designed to extend child-initiated learning, in which the children use the role-play areas for their own purposes. Such child-initiated learning might include the use of technology and 'pretend' technology and will provide evidence of the children's ability to transfer learning from the adult-led activities into their own play environment.

Each role play unit is intended to be used flexibly and could last for half a term, about 5 to 6 weeks, depending on the extent to which you wish to develop the activities suggested.

The nature of socio-dramatic or fantasy play

'Well-planned play … is a key way in which young children learn with enjoyment and challenge.' (DfEE/QCA (2000) *Curriculum Guidance for the foundation stage*, p. 25)

In playing children explore the environment in a random and complex way, testing ideas, experimenting with feelings and relationships while developing skills and competence in a range of areas. Socio dramatic role-play involves children in developing make-believe scenarios and requires children to develop an understanding of roles and how to negotiate roles with others.

"Socio-dramatic play enables exploration, whereas directed play enables mastery". (Moyles, J. (1994) *The Excellence of Play*, Open University Press). It is important therefore for children that they are allowed "free" play in between structured play sessions to enable them to consolidate their learning thereby developing both an interactive and experiential curriculum. The role-play mini-units adopt this approach. Teachers can enter the play situation and make the children think more deeply about the way they represent their experiences either by using props, technology, new words or more clearly defined roles, e.g. "what would happen if you go into space?" "What would you need to wear?" "What might you see?"

Socio-dramatic play is important because it:
- feeds the child's imagination
- keeps the brain primed and active in an exploratory mode
- helps develop internal thinking structures and conceptual links between different experiences
- helps acceptance and exploration of new experiences by building upon situations that are related to real life, and which involve technology
- allows children to rehearse situations, make choices and problem solve
- develops empathy by children taking on other roles and developing an awareness of self
- involves communication and negotiation
- is enjoyable and social.

Other components

Flipover Book and Key Questions
These elements offer you the opportunity to present the learning intention for the week in a colourful and interesting way, without the need for the children to be grouped around a computer screen. The Flipover Book follows the concept of a Big Book page and is designed to link with literacy in terms of levels of language and vocabulary used. It provides a challenge for the children to meet in solving a problem for a character or in helping to correct mistakes made in the work presented to them visually. The Key Questions (situated at the back of the Teacher's Book) focus you on the learning intentions for the week, and help you to develop discussion about the skills and techniques which the children will learn, and their other potential uses.

Resource Sheets
In some lessons, the children will need one of the Resource Sheets to help them to prepare for their computer task. For example, they may need to practise an activity on paper before using the computer. These sheets are available as photocopiable material, and the children are shown how to complete them and what their uses are. For example, they may compare a cutting, sticking

activity to using drag and drop on the computer. Other resource sheets are extension tasks for the more able.

Target Sheets
Each week, the children will have clear learning intentions presented at the beginning of the lesson and on their Work Cards. At the end of the lesson, they have a Target Sheet to complete from the Resource File. This consists of a series of "can do" statements related to the skills they have been learning. It will help you to focus on where to offer more support, or where to move the children on to extension tasks.

Flashcards
Each lesson has a series of cards containing specialist vocabulary relating to the tasks in hand. You are able to photocopy these cards from the Resource File and display them in the classroom as a reminder to the children of new areas of skills which they are developing.

Work Cards
The Work Cards are in a four-page format. Page one outlines the targets for the week, with illustrated support and a clear task set for completion during the week. The inside pages of the Work Card have screenshots of the software program the children will be using, together with a step-by-step guide on which buttons to press to tell the computer what they want it to do. Non-specialists can use these cards to try out the skills before the lesson and increase their own confidence. Page four of the Work Card offers possible follow-up tasks at the same level as those on page one, for those who finish early or who need more practice with the particular skill.

CD-ROM
Where a lesson requires you, for example, to use a particular text, or to have a picture available for the children to change or edit, you will find a sample on CD-ROM to save you time in preparation. Where extra screens will help the children to gain more confidence with possible applications of their skills, they have been designed and included on CD-ROM. For younger children in Reception/P1, the CD-ROM

offers opportunities to engage in more depth with the computer skills by providing a wider range of visual material for them to use.

Teacher's Support

The lesson plan in the Teacher's Book forms the primary source of teacher support for the course. This double page spread offers you everything you need to be able to teach the lesson. Where you feel less confident with your own computer skills, there are additional support pages which give you more background information about the software being used. These pages also contain basic information, such as how to set up your class folders, for example, so that your own skills increase as you move through the course. The support pages also contain a glossary of all key technical vocabulary.

Granada Toolkit

An arrangement has been made with Granada Learning, a successful educational software provider, to use their *Granada Toolkit* in the course materials.

Each element of the *Granada Toolkit* has been designed to meet the requirements of the Programme of Study and the *5–14 National Guidelines* for ICT, and written by teachers and advisers with a wide experience of successful classroom practice.

The icons used in each part of the *Granada Toolkit* relate very clearly to Microsoft's software and are an excellent preparation for children in primary school to enable them to move on to *Word* or *Excel*.

In addition, the Pupil CD-ROM includes some simple activities with functionality designed to give children experience of simple techniques such as "clicking and pointing" and key ICT ideas – for example, that sounds and pictures can convey information.

Long-, medium- and short-term planning

The units in each year of the *Nelson Thornes Primary ICT* scheme prepare the children for work based on the QCA documentation. Each school's long-term plan will link with its overall curriculum plan, taking into account the needs of all children. The overview to each unit shows possible links which teachers may make in each six-week block, in order to integrate their IT teaching into their school's curriculum map. The units may be taught in a different order over the year, but completion of them ensures a variety of IT experiences.

Each six-week unit of work within the *Nelson Thornes Primary ICT* scheme forms the basis of the medium-term plan, where clear learning objectives are given for the half term, which promote progression within a skills' area, show the resources needed, and estimate the time needed to acquire the targeted skills. The medium-term plan also shows clearly how teachers may assess the level of competence of each child with the skills outlined at the beginning of the unit. Exemplars of assessment sheets are given at the end of the Resource File.

In the short term, each lesson gives activities and Resource Sheets which will enable the children to reach the stated targets. The scheme gives lists of resources and suggests advance planning activities so that teachers make the best use of their time in the classroom.

Curriculum Guidance for the Foundation Stage

Curriculum Guidance for the Foundation Stage includes many references to the planned use of ICT in the Foundation Stage. The Guidelines suggest that children should be given opportunities:
- "to gather information to satisfy their curiosity"
- "to use CD-ROMs to follow up questions and find new information"
- "to complete a simple program on the computer and/or perform simple functions on ICT apparatus"
- "to find out about everyday technology and use ICT and programmable toys to support their learning".

Nelson Thornes Primary ICT offers opportunities for children to develop ICT skills and explore all of these areas in focused activities or role-play situations.

5–14 National Guidelines for ICT

Links between *Nelson Thornes Primary ICT P1* and the *5–14 National Guidelines* (Learning and Teaching Scotland, 2000) are provided on page 105. Links to all of the key aspects of the Curriculum Framework for Children 3 to 5 (SCCC, 1999) are also supplied on page 106 covering the role-play activities in Unit 4.

Assessment

Lessons have clear learning objectives, making assessment easier and more manageable to set up. How is the assessment carried out, and how is it linked with the Foundation Stage/P1? Each lesson contains a Pupil Target Sheet with a list of "can-do" statements linked with the learning intentions for the week. These "single" lesson targets build into a "unit" target every six weeks. Each lesson, in addition, provides a list of the opportunities teachers have to assess the children's success in meeting their targets, including plenary discussion, completed computer tasks and completed Pupil Target Sheets.

Continuity and Progression

Nelson Thornes Primary ICT has a clear structure of units in six-week blocks. In Reception/P1 the units ensure a progressive development of skills relevant to children aged 3–5. Each unit has at the beginning an outline of the development of skills over the six weeks and sets the current work into context, showing teachers how it relates to what the children have done previously and what they will do later in the Key Stage. The progression of skills is mapped out for teachers and provides effective guidelines for levels to be attempted in each unit. Work Cards which focus on the skills to be developed may be left constantly available at the computer so that children who are unsure may re-visit any of the six lessons at their own pace. In addition each unit provides guidelines for links with key skills, including thinking skills.

Differentiation

Each lesson contained within the Teacher's Book is aimed at the pre-skills required to prepare the children to operate within the QCA guidance in Key Stage 1. In order to meet the needs of more able children, extra Resource Sheets are available to enable them to attempt work at a higher level. The Work Cards have a "follow-up" section which consolidates the skills targeted for that week and helps children who find the work difficult at first. Teachers receive further guidance in the "Watchpoints" section of each lesson to help them to reinforce and re-visit areas where the children have problems.

Using ICT across the curriculum

Children first of all need skills in using a computer. They need to know how things work and how to input data accurately in order to achieve the results they are seeking. Teachers, therefore, need to provide these skills in a clear and progressively more complex fashion in order to empower children to solve increasingly complex problems. *Nelson Thornes Primary ICT* provides opportunities for children to do this in an interesting way, always within a context which will at the same time help them to develop their skills in other subjects. Once the children have learned the skills, and the area of their other subject to which those skills are relevant, they may start to apply them more independently. This is particularly the case in numeracy and literacy.

The role-play activities in Unit 4 offer particular opportunities to consolidate and apply the key ICT skills and techniques using structured play and an interactive cross-curricular environment. Links between these activities and all of the key aspects of the foundation stage are supplied on pages 106.

Nelson Thornes Primary

ICT

LESSON PLANS

Words and pictures

 Lesson ▼ **•••• UNIT MAP**

1	• To understand that the mouse controls the pointer • To be able to use a mouse with a degree of hand and eye co-ordination • To be able to use ICT to match words and pictures
2	• To understand that words convey information • To understand that text comes in different sizes, colours and styles • To learn that text can be entered into a computer and printed out • To recognise familiar names, and letters on a keyboard
3	• To recognise familiar letters on a keyboard • To learn that single letters can be entered into the computer • To understand that text can be entered into a computer and printed out
4	• To recognise familiar letters on a keyboard • To be able to type CVC words with the support of words and pictures
5	• To understand that ICT can be used to assemble text • To select text from a word list • To select and listen to text using a mouse
6	• To be able to produce text on screen that is clear and error-free

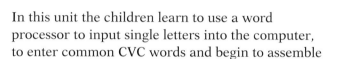 **About this unit** ▼

In this unit the children learn to use a word processor to input single letters into the computer, to enter common CVC words and begin to assemble simple text using a word list.

They discuss how words in the environment convey information. They begin to discuss writing for a purpose.

Lesson 1 can be used to identify children's earlier experiences of using a computer at home or in their nursery classes. The lesson offers some ready-made activities requiring the children to select and move items on screen. This will enable you to observe whether the children are yet able to use the mouse to control the pointer and whether they can use it with a degree of hand and eye co-ordination. Some children may require additional practice in using the mouse to make selections on the screen before moving on to the other lessons in this unit.

Integrated tasks and links ▼

The application of the skills learned here is wide. You may wish to put them into operation in your current planning.

Communication and language: this unit links directly to the Early Learning Goal for Communication, language and literacy and to the key aspect, Communication and Language, in the *Curriculum Framework for children 3 to 5*, as follows: The children are encouraged to recognise and type the letters of their own name along with other simple words for labels and captions. They begin to form simple sentences with help. They attempt writing for different purposes, including simple letter writing. They use their phonetic knowledge to find initial sounds and write CVC words. They match words (for example, words that rhyme). They read a range of familiar and common words, exploring and experimenting with sounds, words and texts in the context of play experiences. They express thoughts with increasing confidence and use talk to organise and clarify their thinking. They sustain attentive listening, responding to what they have seen and heard with relevant comments, questions and actions.

Knowledge and understanding of the world: the children are encouraged to find out and talk about their environment by looking for words/text. They comment and ask questions and develop their powers of observation by matching text and pictures.

Physical development: the children will develop fine motor control through the use of the computer mouse.

.

Skills progression ▼

This is an introductory unit. Lesson 1 can be used to find out whether children can identify simple words and pictures on screen and use a mouse with some degree of control. The rest of the unit builds on these skills and uses them to assemble text and pictures with increasing confidence.

The unit then forms a line of progression in assembling text and organising pictures. The children go on to develop these skills in Year 1/P2 Unit 2 "Using a word bank", where they develop their keyboard skills and use the word and clip art bank facilities in *Granada Writer* to assemble sentences and pictures that communicate meaning.

Key words ▼

Prepare flashcards to display around the room to remind the children, during the week, of the specialist vocabulary they may need. The key words can be found in the Reception/P1 Resources File and can be enlarged to A3 size on a photocopier.

Lesson 1 ▶	mouse, control, pointer, screen, print, printer, keyboard, click
Lesson 2 ▶	key, keyboard, text, shift key, backspace, mouse, screen, print, printer
Lesson 3 ▶	keyboard, keys, space bar, text, type
Lesson 4 ▶	backspace, delete, keys, keyboard, text, type
Lesson 5 ▶	match, mouse, word list, screen, keyboard, find
Lesson 6 ▶	word list, find, delete, print, printer, backspace

UNIT 1

Words and pictures

Overview 2 ▼

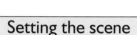

Setting the scene ▼

1 Red Ted's ship

Red Ted is introduced. The children help him to tidy his ship.
They focus upon control of the mouse through good hand and eye co-ordination. They create a picture of Red Ted's ship by moving objects around the screen and labelling certain objects with prepared text. The activity requires the children to point and click to move an object and click again to place the object in position.

2 Labels and signs

Red Ted makes a label with his hame on it.
Children learn that words convey information. They talk about words/text they see around them, for example, labels, signs, what they mean and why they are there, and how text is presented in different sizes, colours and styles. The children produce a name label to use at school, perhaps to label a book, drawer or a picture on the wall.

3 Red Ted finds treasure

Red Ted finds a treasure chest around which there are letters attached to keys.
The children must find the letters on the keyboard to match the letters around the treasure chest. The children begin to use the keyboard to find the position of different letters. They have the opportunity to "play" writing using the keyboard.

.

Special resources and advanced planning

You will need to be familiar with the functions of the computer listed in the unit map. Spend some time each week before each lesson in familiarising yourself with those functions. You may find it useful to work through the children's Work Cards as well.

Lesson 1 ▶ Have labels ready for all the movable items in Red Ted's cabin (to match those on the data file) and for each part of the computer from Resource Sheet 1: screen, keyboard, mouse, cursor, computer. See Teacher's Support section for how to make a label template.

Lesson 2 ▶ Prepare a template for the children's labels. Check there are labels and signs around the classroom. Make an A3 size keyboard which is mounted on card and laminated. See Teacher's Support section for info on how to do both these things.

4   Red Ted has a pet

Red Ted is in the pet shop looking for another pet.
All the pictures of animals are to be labelled. They are common CVC words. Children enter CVC words into the computer to match the pictures they see on the screen. Children develop familiarity with the letters on the keyboard. A simpler version of the data file exists, where the names of the animals are already in place and the children simply copy them.

5   Red Ted plays a game

Red Ted is playing a game that involves matching pictures to words like a jigsaw.
The children play a similar game on the computer where they match words to pictures. In this lesson the children use a simple word list to input text into the computer. They discuss and compare the two ways of inputting text: typing and using a word list.

6   Red Ted writes a letter

Red Ted writes a letter to the children.
The children write a letter about themselves to send back to Red Ted. They produce a simple piece of personal text using a word list to insert key words. The children are encouraged to listen to the words and sentences to check they make sense. To extend the activity into other areas of the curriculum the children could write to Red Ted about something they are learning related to their topic.

 Lesson 3 ▶ You will need your card keyboard or spare keyboard.

 Lesson 4 ▶ You will need your card keyboard or spare keyboard.

Lesson 5 ▶ Picture dictionaries, jigsaws that match words and pictures, a set of pictures and words that match the game on the computer: flag, map, bed, pen. These could be printed from the computer.

Lesson 6 ▶ A letter sent from Red Ted which will be read to the class. The letter contains simple text about Red Ted, such as "My name is Red Ted. I am five years old. I am a pirate. I like to sail in my boat." The letter should contain conventions such as address, date, "Dear children," and "love Red Ted". The letter should be in an airmail envelope as it will have been sent from abroad.

UNIT 1

Red Ted's ship

Lesson 1 ▼

Learning intentions ▼

- To understand that the mouse controls the pointer
- To be able to use a mouse with a degree of hand and eye co-ordination
- To be able to use ICT to match words and pictures

Resources and setting up ▼

- Flipover Book page 1 and Key Questions
- Resource Sheet 1 (extension only)
- Resource Sheet 2 (extension only)
- Target Sheet 1 (one each)
- Work Card 1
- **Ship** data file
- *Granada Colours* (optional)

▼ Keywords

| Lesson 1 ▶ | mouse, control, pointer, screen, print, printer, keyboard, click |

▼ Activities

Introduction whole class

- Introduce the children to Red Ted, the pirate. Explain that they are going to use a computer to help him tidy his ship.

- Use the Flipover Book page and Key Questions to introduce the idea that pictures and words on a computer screen can be manipulated using the mouse.

- Go back to the Flipover Book page and discuss how it is impossible to tidy the picture because objects cannot be moved. Tell the children that on the computer objects can be moved. WP1

- Show the children the prepared labels you have made. Ask the children to read the word with you and ask one child to put the label onto the matching picture on the Flipover Book page. WP2

Getting started whole class or groups

- Open the **Ship** data file, which shows the same picture as on the Flipover Book page.

- Tell the children that they are going to help Red Ted tidy his ship by moving the objects around.

- Discuss how this is achieved by moving the pointer to the object, clicking and then pointing to where the object is to be moved.

- Show the children the flashcards "mouse", "pointer", "screen" and "control".

- Go over the idea of control, as this is central to the activity and to future work on a computer.

- Demonstrate control by moving objects around the screen.

- Show the children Work Card 1, and use it to explain the computer task.

At the computer individual/pairs with adult support

● Support each child in opening the **Ship** data file and saving it to their folder as "their name + Ship". WP3

● The children use Work Card 1 to move the objects around the room by clicking on each object and pointing to where it should be moved. A second click positions the object on the screen. WP4

● Each child should be encouraged to make decisions about where each object should be placed and then move the object with the mouse. WP5

● Make sure each child prints out the finished picture using the print button. Some children will work on a follow up activity to match labels to the pictures on screen.

● Extension: some children will use Resource Sheets 1 and 2 to reinforce the key vocabulary of the lesson and to encourage them to start to think about the position of the letters on the keyboard.

Plenary whole class

● Use the Flipover Book page, Key Questions and the children's own work to talk about how the computer allows them to move words and pictures around the screen.

● Stress the need for control of the mouse in order to create the desired effect. WP6

● Complete the Target Sheets together.

● Tell the children that in the next session they will learn a little more about signs and labels and how the computer can be used to create them.

WP1 Use the end of the Key Questions session to explore children's understanding of how objects can be moved on screen. Have any of the children used the mouse before? What did they do with it? etc. Explain that they will use the mouse to move the objects and add labels to each one.

WP2 See the *Advanced planning and special resources* section at the beginning of this unit. These labels can also be used in the extension task, though the children may need adult support to read and place the labels. It is important to reinforce this key vocabulary throughout the unit.

WP3 For information on saving the children's work see the Teacher's Support section.

WP4 Control of the mouse requires good hand and eye co-ordination and it is an important skill to develop. If children are experiencing problems with this, support the child by placing your hand over his/hers on the mouse as you guide the pointer around the screen.

WP5 Encourage the children to "play" with the picture and experiment with placing the objects in different places until they are happy with the finished look.

WP6 Some work using the Shapes bank in *Granada Colours* would be useful for those children who continue to have problems with mouse control.

- Discussion of use of mouse to move objects on screen (from Introduction)

- Printed picture (from Work Card task)

- Ability to explain how they moved objects using the mouse (from Plenary)

- Completed Resource Sheets

- Completed Target Sheet

Labels and signs

Lesson 2 ▼

Learning intentions ▼

- To understand that words convey information
- To understand that text comes in different sizes, colours and styles
- To learn that text can be entered into a computer and printed out
- To recognise familiar names, and letters on a keyboard

Resources and setting up ▼

- Flipover Book page 2 and Key Questions
- Resource Sheet 3 (one each)
- Resource Sheet 4 (extension only)
- Target Sheet 2 (one each)
- Work Card 2
- **Labels** data file
- Template for preparing labels
- A3 card keyboard or play keyboard

▼ Keywords

Lesson 2 ▶   key, keyboard, text, shift key, backspace, mouse, screen, print, printer

▼ Activities

Introduction whole class

- Remind the children of last week's lesson where they used the computer to manipulate objects on the screen.

- Use the Flipover Book page and Key Questions to introduce the idea that words convey meaning and to encourage the children to look around their environment for labels and signs.

- Explain to the children that they are going to make a label for Red Ted on the computer. They are going to type his name into the computer to make a label for their books. WP1

- Refer back to the Flipover Book page and look again at the labels with "Red Ted" on them.

Getting started whole class

- Open your prepared labels template, with a text box on the screen.

- Tell the children that the writing is going to be big. Ask them why this might be.

- Show the children how to put the cursor into the text box to begin writing.

- Discuss the need for a capital letter and demonstrate how to hold down the shift key. WP1

- Show the children the keys on the prepared card keyboard. Show the Flashcards "key" and "keyboard". WP2

- Show the children how to press the keys lightly but firmly to enter Red Ted's name and demonstrate by typing in a name.

- Show the children how to use the backspace key if they make a mistake.

- Go over all of these keys by showing them on the card keyboard and give each child a copy of Resource Sheet 3 to complete before moving on to the computer task.

WP1 If you prefer you can show them the caps lock key, which would need to be pressed twice – once before the initial capital is pressed and once after. Children should have had some experience of using capital letters for the start of their own names in sentence level work before tackling this computer task.

WP2 You might wish to make these keys stand out by labelling them or making them a different colour. Alternatively, a play keyboard such as *Keyboard Crazy* could be used for demonstration purposes. See Teacher's Support section.

WP3 The label created can be used for any purpose that is appropriate at the time, such as a label for a picture, a book or a drawer. Depending upon the child, they can write their first name only or both first and surname. Using an A4 sheet of paper you may wish the child to make two labels or two children enter labels on one sheet.

WP4 You will need to support them in opening the **Labels** data file and saving it to their folder as "their name + Labels".

WP5 Throughout this unit encourage the children to use the computer with an empty screen to do emergent writing. This will develop their keyboard skills and familiarity with the position of the letters.

At the computer individuals/pairs with adult support

- The children open the prepared labels template. Using Work Card 2 and the completed Resource Sheet 3, the children type Red Ted's name into the text box.

- Each child should be encouraged to look carefully at the keyboard to locate each letter of the name.

- Support each child in using the shift key for the initial capital letter.

- Some children will complete a follow up task to practise making labels typing their own name this time. WP3

- Print out each label. The children can cut out and decorate their labels before using them.

- Extension: some children will use Resource Sheet 4 and the **Labels** data file to type in labels for a series of pictures. WP4

Plenary whole class

- Use the Flipover Book page, Key Questions and the children's own work to talk about how words convey meaning.

- Ask the children to look for labels and signs at home.

- Encourage the children to look at the card keyboard and real keyboard to familiarise themselves with where the letters are. WP5

- Complete the Target Sheets together.

- Tell the children that in the next lesson they will learn a little more about the keyboard.

- Discussion in whole group and in individual/paired activity (from Introduction and Work Card task)

- Printed copy of name (from Work Card task)

- Ability to explain what their label is for (from Plenary)

- Completed Resource Sheets

- Completed Target Sheet

Red Ted finds treasure

Learning intentions ▼

- To recognise familiar letters on a keyboard
- To learn that single letters can be entered into the computer
- To understand that text can be entered into a computer and printed out

Resources and setting up ▼

- Flipover Book page 3 and Key Questions
- Resource Sheet 5 (extension only)
- Target Sheet 3 (one each)
- Work Card 3
- **Treasure 1** and **Treasure 2** data files

▼ Keywords

Lesson 3 ▶	keyboard, keys, space bar, text, type

▼ Activities

Introduction whole class

- Remind the children about last week's lesson where they were getting familiar with the keyboard.
- Tell the children that in this lesson they will extend their ability to find particular letters on the keyboard.
- Tell the children that Red Ted has found a map of a treasure island. He has used it to find some treasure, but he needs help to open it.
- Use the Flipover Book page and Key Questions to introduce the lesson.
- Locate the letters on the Flipover Book page on the card keyboard. WP1

Getting started whole class

- Tell the children that they are going to use Red Ted's special letters on the computer.
- Open the **Treasure 1** data file. On the screen you will see a picture of Red Ted and his treasure chest from the Flipover Book page.
- Tell the children that they need to find the right letters to open the chest. When they find a letter they click on it to hear the sound it makes. WP2
- Demonstrate by clicking on a letter.
- Explain that next they need to find that letter on the keyboard and press the key.
- Ask a child to find the key and press. Explain that once all the letters have been clicked on, the chest will open and Red Ted will find the treasure!
- Show the children Work Card 3 which supports them in their task. Check that they all understand what they have to do.

Watchpoints ▼

WP1   It would be useful here to help the children, for example, by saying that the required letter is on the bottom row in the middle of the keyboard. As an alternative, a play keyboard could be used for demonstration purposes.

WP2   The children should be encouraged to take turns to press the keys during this activity and discuss the position of each letter.

WP3   The children are encouraged to "play" with letters and see the results of pressing keys and entering letters. The children may prompt discussion of the need to use the space bar and the back space or delete keys.

WP4   See Teacher's Support section for more information on this.

At the computer pairs

● Support each child in opening the **Treasure 1** data file and saving it to their folder as "their name + Treasure 1".

● Using Work Card 3, the children search for the letters on the screen to make and type the word "open". WP2

● The children will then move on to a follow up task to use the **Treasure 2** data file to type the names of the different types of treasure that Red Ted has found. WP3

● Extension: some children will work on Resource Sheet 5 which shows Red Ted and his treasure chest. The children colour the letters and find them on the keyboard.

Plenary whole class

● Using the Flipover Book page, Key Questions and completed Resource Sheet, discuss the use of the keyboard and the position of the letters.

● Look at some of the "emergent writing" done on the computer in the follow up and extension task and talk with the children about how they managed with the tasks.

● Tell the children that it is important that when they are typing on a keyboard they use more than one finger.

● Demonstrate on the card keyboard how to use all fingers as good practice. WP4

● Complete the Target Sheets together.

● Tell the children that next week they will be typing more words onto the computer and helping Red Ted find another pet.

Assessment of learning outcomes ▼

● Ability to locate particular keys (from Work Card task and follow up task)

● Discussion of activity (from Introduction)

● Print out of data files (from Work Card task)

● Completed Resource Sheet

● Completed Target Sheet

Red Ted has a pet

Learning intentions ▼
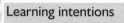

- To recognise familiar letters on a keyboard
- To be able to type CVC words with the support of words and pictures

Resources and setting up ▼
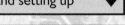

- Flipover Book page 4 and Key Questions
- Resource Sheet 6 (extension only)
- Target Sheet 4 (one each)
- Work Card 4
- **Pets 1**, **Pets 2** and **Red Ted's pet** data files

▼ Keywords

Lesson 4 ▶	backspace, delete, keys, keyboard, text, type,

▼ Activities

Introduction whole class

- Remind the children of last week's lesson where they were getting more familiar with the keyboard. Remind the children that the letters on the keyboard are in upper case. WP1

- Tell the children that in this lesson they will extend their ability to write simple words using the keyboard.

- Use the Flipover Book page and Key Questions to introduce the lesson. Explain that Red Ted wants another pet to keep his ginger cat company.

Getting started whole class

- Tell the children that they are going to make a list of all the pets in the shop for Red Ted to take home to remind him. They will enter each name into the computer.

- Open the data file **Pets 1** which shows pictures of the pets available.

- Using Work Card 4, guide the children through the task.

- Tell the children that the computer will show them a pet with its name written alongside.

- The children need to copy the word into the space provided by finding the keys on the keyboard. WP2

- Remind the children that a firm press is needed, and if they enter an incorrect letter, how to delete using the backspace key.

- Show the children briefly the "picture only" option on **Pets 2**.

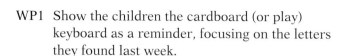

WP1 Show the children the cardboard (or play) keyboard as a reminder, focusing on the letters they found last week.

WP2 Demonstrate this by finding the letters on the keyboard and pressing each one firmly but lightly. You can use both the cardboard (or play) keyboard and/or the real keyboard. See Teacher's Support section.

WP3 You should select the amount of support needed for the children. **Pets 1** includes word and picture clues. **Pets 2** includes picture clues only. Children can do both tasks if appropriate.

WP4 Children should take turns at entering names. Encourage the children to sound out each pet name as they are writing. A word typed correctly is spoken. A word incorrectly typed receives a "try again" prompt.

At the computer pairs

- Select which task is appropriate for the particular pair of children. WP3

- Support each child in opening the **Pets 1** or **Pets 2** data file and saving it to their folder as "their name + Pets 1" (or Pets 2).

- Children work together to type in the name of each pet, discussing the letters and helping each other to locate them on the keyboard. WP4

- When all four animals have been named the list can be printed.

- Read through the list and ask which pet they think Red Ted should have.

- Some children will complete a follow up task to make a sentence using the **Red Ted's pet** data file.

- Extension: some children will progress to the picture only option on **Pets 2** so that they are sounding out the word themselves.

- Children who began with **Pets 2** can use Resource Sheet 6 to draw a picture of Red Ted with his preferred pet and to label it.

Plenary whole class

- Use the Flipover Book page, Key Questions and printouts to look at CVC words.

- Discuss with the children that writing on a computer can sometimes make words easier to read, but that it takes time because you need to know where all the letters are.

- Complete the Target Sheets together.

- Tell the children that in the next lesson they will use the computer to write, using a method that is quicker.

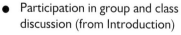

Assessment of learning outcomes ▼

- Participation in group and class discussion (from Introduction)

- Ability to use keyboard (from Work Card task)

- Printout of list (from Work Card task)

- Completed Resource Sheet

- Completed Target Sheet

Red Ted plays a game

Lesson 5 ▼

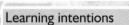

Learning intentions ▼

- To understand that ICT can be used to assemble text
- To select text from a word list
- To select and listen to text using a mouse

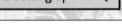

Resources and setting up ▼

- Flipover Book page 5 and Key Questions
- Resource Sheet 7 (one each)
- Resource Sheet 8 (extension only)
- Target Sheet 5 (one each)
- Work Card 5
- **Pictures** data file

▼ Keywords

Lesson 5 ▶	match, mouse, word list, screen, keyboard, find

▼ Activities

Introduction whole class

- Remind the children of last week's lesson where they were entering CVC words into the computer.
- Tell the children that in this lesson they will look at how the computer can help them with their writing.
- Use the Flipover Book page and Key Questions to introduce today's lesson about matching words and pictures. WP1

Getting started whole class

- Tell the children they will be playing a similar game on the computer.
- Open the **Pictures** data file, which shows a selection of pictures and text boxes into which the children will enter the correct word to match the picture. To the right of the pictures there is a word list.
- Focus on the word list. Explain to the children that instead of typing in words they can select a word from the list. WP2
- Explain that the computer will speak the words if you press the sound icon.
- Now focus on one of the pictures on the screen. Ask the children what they can see.
- Show them how to find the matching word in the word list, listening to the words.
- Show the children how to enter words into the text box by selecting the chosen word then clicking into the text box.
- Show the children Work Card 5 which guides them through the activity and make sure they all understand what they have to do.

WP1 If you have any similar jigsaws in the classroom you may wish to show them after your discussion about the Flipover Book picture.

WP2 If you have some kind of word list in the classroom make reference to this as a way of finding words.

WP3 You could ask the children what the word says prior to hearing it spoken. The children could use clues from initial sounds. All the words should be familiar to the children from previous lessons.

WP4 The children should be encouraged to listen to all the words before making a selection. For children requiring further support, prepare Resource Sheet 7. This will enable children to play the game manually before completing it in the computer task.

WP5 You will need to set the font size so the labels print out at an appropriate size.

At the computer pairs

● Support each child in opening the **Pictures** data file and saving it to their folder as "their name + Pictures".

● Using Work Card 5, the children use the word list to complete the activity with support from both the words and pictures. WP4

● The children should be encouraged to use the "listen" function and to talk about the pictures they can see.

● Some children will complete the follow up task to remember the names of the pictures when they are presented in a different order.

● Extension: some children will use Resource Sheet 8 to write labels for a different set of pictures. WP5

Plenary whole class

● Use the Flipover Book page and Key Questions to establish how confidently the children are able to match words and pictures.

● Discuss with the children how the computer allowed them to enter words onto the screen by selecting them from the word list rather than typing them in.

● Compare the two ways of entering text.

● Complete the Target Sheets together.

● Discuss how listening to the words helped to select the right word.

● Explain that next week Red Ted will write a letter to the children and that they will write a letter back to him.

Assessment of learning outcomes ▼

- Discussion during whole class and paired work (from Introduction and Work Card task)

- Ability to use the sound icon (from Work Card task)

- Printout of activity (from Work Card task)

- Completed Resource Sheets

- Completed Target Sheet

Red Ted writes a letter

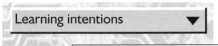
Lesson 6 ▼

Learning intentions ▼

- To be able to produce text on screen that is clear and error-free

Resources and setting up ▼

- Flipover Book page 6 and Key Questions
- Resource Sheet 9 (extension only)
- Target Sheet 6 (one each)
- End of Unit Target Sheet (one each)
- Work Card 6
- **Letter** data file

▼ Keywords

Lesson 6 ▶	word list, find, delete, print, printer, backspace

▼ Activities

Introduction whole class

- Remind the children of last week's lesson where they used a word list on the screen.

- Use the Flipover Book page and Key Questions to introduce today's activity.

- Tell the children that a special letter has come today. It is from Red Ted. Read the letter and let the children comment.

- Show the children examples of other letters/correspondence. WP1

Getting started whole class

- Tell the children they are going to write a short letter to Red Ted.

- Tell them they will use Red Ted's letter to help them.

- Re-read Red Ted's letter from the Flipover Book page.

- Write on the board as you rehearse with the children what they will write. WP2

- Open the **Letter** data file.

- Talk about how the letter should start with "Dear Red Ted".

- Tell the children that the computer will help them write the letter.

- Show the children Work Card 6 which guides them through the activity. Make sure that they all understand what they have to do.

Watchpoints ▼

WP1 A range of correspondence could be shown, either real or prepared, especially for this activity e.g. letters, flyers, bills, postcards.

WP2 You should use the same sentences as in Red Ted's letter.

WP3 Children should have the support of an adult during the computer task to help them rehearse the sentences.

At the computer pairs with adult support

● Support each child in opening the **Letter** data file and saving it to their folder as "their name + Letter".

● The children listen to each word in the word list clicking on the sound icon. WP3

● They rehearse with each other and an adult what they will write, using the prompts given on the Work Card.

● The children should be encouraged to enter text using the keyboard and the word list.

● Remind the children about the use of the full stop.

● Each copy printed can be illustrated with a picture of themselves.

● Extension: some children will use Resource Sheet 9 to cut out words and make sentences.

Plenary whole class

● Use the Flipover Book page and Key Questions to reflect upon the objectives of this lesson and the unit as a whole.

● Recap each Flipover picture to reflect upon the tasks achieved, the purpose of the tasks and how the computer has supported the children's learning of writing.

● Complete the Target Sheets together and allow time for the children to complete their End of Unit Target Sheets.

● Put all the letters into an envelope ready to send to Red Ted.

● Explain that next week they will be starting a new unit on information.

Assessment of learning outcomes ▼

● Participation in whole class and group discussion (from Introduction)

● Ability to use a word list (from Work Card task and Plenary)

● Print out of letter (from Work Card task)

● Completed Resource Sheet

● Completed Target Sheet

● Completed End of Unit Target Sheet

UNIT 2

Presenting information

 •••• **UNIT MAP**

I	• To show awareness that information comes from a variety of sources • To be able to complete a simple program on the computer • To show an awareness of change
2	• To understand that sounds convey information • To be able to use a tape recorder to record and store information as sound • To be able to match sounds to pictures
3	• To understand that pictures and text convey information • To show curiosity, observe and manipulate objects using ICT
4	• To understand that moving pictures convey information • To perform a simple function on ICT apparatus
5	• To recognise how text, pictures, icons and sound are used in a computer program • To be able to use a talking book with confidence
6	• To understand that information can be presented in a variety of forms and collected from a variety of sources • To be able to use a simple paint package or writing package

About this unit ▼

This is an introductory unit that provides children with a range of experiences that begin to develop their knowledge and understanding of the fact that information exists all around them in a variety of forms. The unit can also be used to develop children's general awareness of the everyday uses of technology. Finally, the children are encouraged to reflect upon their everyday experiences, to identify different forms of information they encounter on a daily basis.

They learn that information can be presented as text, still and moving pictures, sounds and multimedia. They will begin to discuss, reflect upon and compare the way information is presented.

They learn that different types of media are used to give different types of information and that ICT can be used to manipulate information.

Lesson 1 uses the theme of the weather to identify children's awareness of the ways in which information is presented – in print, on the television or radio, through a computer, and so on. This lesson can be used to assess whether children are ready to move on to presenting information themselves using different media.

Integrated tasks and links ▼

The application of the skills learned here is wide. You may wish to put them into operation in your current planning.

Communication and language: this unit links directly to the Early Learning Goal for Communication, language and literacy and to the key aspect, Communication and Language, in the *Curriculum Framework for children 3 to 5*, as follows:

The children have opportunities to interact with others, negotiating activities and taking turns in conversations. They will listen to stories and respond to what they have heard. They will extend their vocabulary in relation to aspects of ICT and the use of the computer. The activities provide opportunities to use speech to organise and clarify their thinking and ideas when presenting information to others and they will be able to express needs, thoughts and feelings with increasing confidence. They will develop their understanding that print carries meaning and how information can be found in non-fiction texts. When using the talking books, children will extend their reading and comprehension skills. The whole unit encourages the children to interact with environmental print. The children will cover word, sentence and text level work.

Knowledge and understanding of the world: the children's knowledge and understanding of the wider world and local environment are extended through investigation into how information is found, displayed and used for a range of purposes. They begin to study how information about the weather is conveyed in different ways, such as forecasts on the television and maps in the newspapers, and they broaden their awareness of changes in the weather and its effects on them. They are also encouraged to develop skills of enquiry through posing questions. The children could undertake an environmental walk around the school, school grounds or the local area to find information. This unit makes links with the QCA scheme for geography "Where in the World is Barnaby Bear?"

Skills progression ▼

This unit extends children's skills and experience of using software, that is in manipulating the mouse, using the keyboard, entering text into a computer. This unit provides a foundation for Year 1/P2 Unit 3 "Information around us" and Unit 5 "Pictograms".

Key words ▼

Prepare flashcards to display around the room, to remind the children during the week of the specialist vocabulary they may need. The key words can be found in the Reception /P1 Resources File and can be enlarged to A3 size on a photocopier.

Lesson 1 ▶	information, picture, weather map, save
Lesson 2 ▶	sound, information, icon, tape recorder, record, play, listen
Lesson 3 ▶	information, picture, text, tape recorder, play, record, rewind
Lesson 4 ▶	information, video
Lesson 5 ▶	talking book, icon, sound, picture, home, next, back, return
Lesson 6 ▶	information, text, sound, display

Presenting information

Overview 2 ▼

Setting the scene ▼

1 What is the weather like?

Help Red Ted to find out about the weather.
In this lesson the children are introduced to the different ways information is presented, including the use of text, pictures and symbols. The focus of the activity is based upon weather maps and forecasts. The children are encouraged to reflect upon their own experiences inside and outside school and to discuss the information around them. They discuss the information being conveyed and why it is important. The children create a weather map on the computer using symbols and pictures to convey the information. They are encouraged to "present" the forecast to another group of children.

2 What can you hear?

Where is Red Ted? Use the sounds to find out where he is.
In this lesson the children have to guess where Red Ted is by listening to different sounds. They answer by selecting the appropriate picture from a selection on the screen. Several possible answers provide an opportunity for discussion about what information is needed to identify the place. The lesson aims to explore the information sounds give us.

3 Treasure map

Reading Red Ted's map!
This lesson aims to raise awareness that information can be found in different forms. The children discuss how pictures and text convey information. They create a map of an imaginary island and explain how the pictures/icons on the map convey what is on the island and what the island is like.

Special resources and advanced planning

You will need to be familiar with the functions of the computer listed in the unit map. Spend some time each week before each lesson in familiarising yourself with those functions. You may find it useful to work through the children's Work Cards as well.

Lesson 1 ▶

Prepare a collection of different types of information such as a guide book, a recipe book, a cereal box, a picture of traffic lights, a bus timetable. Video examples of weather forecasts from the television and prepare the video in the classroom. Bring in a map of the UK with weather symbols that are the same as those on the CD-ROM. Have ready a large copy of a weather map from a newspaper to show the children, together with simple text for you to read to describe the weather shown.

Lesson 2 ▶

You will need a tape recorder and blank tapes.

4 Red Ted's holiday

Where is Red Ted going for his holidays?
In this lesson the children find out about Red Ted's holidays by exploring pictures. A range of different types of information is provided including video, photographs, pictures of artefacts, postcards and a packed suitcase. The children discuss the pictures to find out about the country Red Ted has visited.

5 Talking stories

Finding out what Red Ted likes to read.
In this lesson the children explore a talking book, in which the information is presented in a variety of forms. They discuss the different ways the information is presented in book form and compare this electronic story with a traditional paper-based version. They explore icons as a way of providing information on a computer.

6 All about...

Making a class display.
In this lesson the children are encouraged to become active in their own learning by way of a topic – All about… (relating to current curriculum planning). They are encouraged to think about what information to collect, where they will find it and how they will present it. The end product will be a display and/or class book. The children are encouraged to collect information in a variety of forms including drawings, photographs, books and interviews.

Lesson 3 ▶
Bring in various holiday brochures, a globe, postcards – a set of postcards with four different images of a place, a passport.

Lesson 4 ▶
Have ready A4 sheets of paper, on which are examples of different font sizes, 12, 28, 72. Collect examples of holiday brochures and postcards. A large globe will also be required for the introductory session.

Lesson 5 ▶
Have ready various types of books to include a school reading book, encyclopaedia, magazine, comic, book on ships, recipe book and dictionary.

Lesson 6 ▶
You will need a display space for the children to use to include the board and table top area. The lesson revolves around an agreed topic related to current planning. The children will need access to different forms of information on this topic. You will need a camera, a tape recorder and blank tapes. Optional requirements are a video recorder, pre-recorded tape of an interview with a pirate (fictional or based upon fact), an information book on, for example, "Our Town", "Our School".

What is the weather like?

Lesson 1

Learning intentions

- To show awareness that information comes from a variety of sources
- To be able to complete a simple program on the computer
- To show an awareness of change

Resources and setting up

- Flipover Book page 7 and Key Questions
- Resource Sheet 10 (one each)
- Resource Sheet 11 (for teacher)
- Target Sheet 7 (one each)
- Work Card 7
- A collection of different types of information e.g. a guide book, a recipe book, a cereal box, a picture of traffic lights, a bus timetable
- **Weather** data file

▼ Keywords

Lesson 1 ▶	information, picture, weather map, save

▼ Activities

Introduction whole class

- Tell the children that this unit is about all the different ways we find out about things.

- Show the children examples of things that give us information, for example recipe books and newspapers. Ask the children if they can think of any others.

- Use the Flipover Book page and Key Questions to introduce the idea that information is important in our everyday lives and can be found all around us. WP1

- Go back to the Flipover Book page and ask the children to think about how they might represent the weather on a map using weather symbols. WP2

- Explain to the children that they are going to make a weather map on the computer to show information about the weather in the United Kingdom. WP3

Getting started whole class

- Open the **Weather** data file on screen.

- Look at the map and symbols and relate this to the example undertaken in the introduction.

- Discuss how to move the weather pictures by moving the pointer to the symbol, clicking and then pointing to where the picture is to be moved.

- Model the language as you move the pictures. (There will be sunny spells in the north. Rain will fall this afternoon. There might be some snow on the high ground.)

- Give each child a copy of Resource Sheet 10, which asks them to think about how weather information is presented.

- Show the children Work Card 7 which provides support during the computer task.

Watchpoints

WP1 When using the Flipover Book page you might want to include a video clip of a weather forecast taken from the television. This will give support to those children who have not had first-hand experience of seeing a weather forecast, in the activities that follow.

WP2 Have a map of the United Kingdom available and indicate where Red Ted's ship is. Have your prepared weather symbols for the children to choose. Resource Sheet 11 includes a set of weather symbols to cut out and use in this introductory session. This activity is developed further as a role play activity in Role play 1 "Television studio" (see page 54 for details).

WP3 This is planned as an imaginary activity. However, more able children might use data from newspapers to create more accurate weather forecasts.

WP4 They may need adult support to do this.

WP5 Work on a paint package such as *Granada Colours* would be useful for those children who continue to have problems with mouse control.

WP6 Make sure children save the CD-ROM activity for this lesson (the **Weather** data file), as they will use it again in Unit 4 Role play 1 "Television studio" (see page 54 for details).

At the computer individuals or pairs with adult support

● Support each child in opening the **Weather** data file and saving it to their folder as "their name + Weather".

● Using Work Card 7, the children move the pictures onto the map to create an imaginary weather map. WP4

● Each child should be encouraged to complete the follow up task, "play" with the weather pictures and to develop a commentary by changing and moving the pictures around. WP5

● Print out the finished map. WP6

● Extension: some children could be encouraged to use more pictures to make their weather forecast more complex, or try to make a weather map showing the day's weather.

Plenary whole class

● Use the Flipover Book page, Key Questions and the children's own work to talk about how information on weather is presented.

● Ask individual children to "role play" weather forecasters to present their maps.

● Reinforce the message that information is all around us and comes from different sources.

● Show the children a range of different types of information, asking them what information is given and why it is important.

● Complete the Target Sheets together.

● Prepare the children for the next lesson by asking what information sound gives us. Ask the children to listen for sounds on the way home and at home.

Assessment of learning outcomes

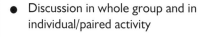

● Discussion in whole group and in individual/paired activity

● Printed weather map (from Work Card task)

● Ability to explain the weather as shown (from follow up task)

● Ability to identify information around him/her

● Completed Resource Sheet

● Completed Target Sheet

What can you hear?

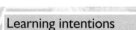
Lesson 2 ▼

Learning intentions ▼

- To understand that sounds convey information
- To be able to use a tape recorder to record and store information as sound
- To be able to match sounds to pictures

Resources and setting up ▼

- Flipover Book page 8 and Key Questions
- Resource Sheet 12 (extension only)
- Target Sheet 8 (one each)
- Work Card 8
- *Granada Writer*
- **Sounds** data file

▼ Keywords

Lesson 2 ▶ sound, information, icon, tape recorder, record, play, listen

▼ Activities

Introduction whole class

- Remind the children of last week's work where they made a weather map using pictures.
- Use the Flipover Book page and Key Questions to introduce children to the idea that information can be conveyed as sound.
- Show the flashcards for the key words.
- Use examples found in school to discuss what sounds can tell us, for example, the school bell tells us that playtime has ended.
- Ask the children to give other examples of sounds from outside school, for example an ambulance. Discuss what the sounds tell us.
- Play the children some of the sounds from the *Granada Writer* sound bank. WP1

Getting started whole class/groups

- Open the **Sounds** data file.
- Discuss the pictures on the screen.
- Ask the children to close their eyes and to try to guess where Red Ted is by listening carefully to the sound. Click on the icon for sound and listen to the first sound you hear. WP2
- Once the sound has been identified ask the children what the sound is telling us/Red Ted. WP3
- Look at Work Card 8 and ask the children to select the picture to go with the sound.
- Show the children how to match each sound with a picture on the screen.

WP1 There are some useful sounds in the Everyday sounds section of the sound bank: alarm clock, baby's rattle, door bell etc.

WP2 If the children cannot guess the sound, move on to the next one and replay the sound later for them to have another go.

WP3 It is important to reinforce that sounds tell us information and the children can, not only identify the sound, but explain its meaning/purpose. You may need to give the children examples of how to answer. (I can hear an ambulance. This tells me that someone is hurt and there is something wrong.)

WP4 Use a simple tape recorder if available. Show the children how to use it and encourage them to think carefully about the sounds they record.

WP5 It is important that you work with the children on the extension task. Ask them to describe their drawings and explore the children's understanding of why these objects make sounds. You might take the extension task further by asking them to find and select pictures and sounds of the objects from *Granada Writer* clip art and sound banks.

At the computer pairs

- Support each child in opening the **Sounds** data file and saving it to their folder as "their name + Sounds".

- Using Work Card 8, the children listen to each sound and discuss what it is and what it tells you about where Red Ted is.

- The children match the sound to Red Ted's location by using both sound and picture clues.

- As a follow up task, some children will record and store sounds using a tape recorder. WP4

- The children should replay and listen to their sounds.

- Extension: some children will use Resource Sheet 12 to encourage them to think of sounds at home and why the sounds are made. WP5

Plenary whole class

- Use the Flipover Book page and the Key Questions to review the way sounds convey information.

- Use some of the children's tape recordings. Ask the children why they selected the particular sounds and what information each sound gives.

- Focus on the task on Resource Sheet 12 and ask the children to talk about the sounds they heard at home.

- Complete the Target Sheets together.

- Explain that next week the children will be looking at how pictures and words give us information.

Assessment of learning outcomes ▼

- Ability to identify sounds (from Work Card task)

- Children's notes on sound/picture matches (from Work Card task)

- Ability to recognise that sounds convey information (from Work Card task)

- Ability to use a tape recorder to record and store information as sound (from follow up task)

- Completed Resource Sheet

- Completed Target Sheet

UNIT 2

Treasure map

Lesson 3 ▼

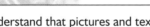

Learning intentions ▼

- To understand that pictures and text convey information
- To show curiosity, observe and manipulate objects using ICT

Resources and setting up ▼

- Flipover Book page 9 and Key Questions
- Resource Sheet 13 (extension only)
- Target Sheet 9 (one each)
- Work Card 9
- **Island** data file
- A collection of different types of information e.g. a guide book, a recipe book, a cereal box, a picture of traffic lights, a bus timetable

▼ Keywords

| **Lesson 3** ▶ | information, picture, text, tape recorder, play, record, rewind |

▼ Activities

Introduction whole class

- Remind the children of last week's work where they looked at information as sound.

- Explain that this week they will be looking at how pictures and words give us information.

- Using the Flipover Book page and Key Questions, discuss what the children can see in the picture. WP1

- Discuss with the children how pictures and words tell us things.

- Show the children examples of pictorial and textual information such as a children's recipe book, a children's gardening book, a toy catalogue, a big information book for children, a poster for a new fiction book, packaging for a new toy, a passport, a holiday brochure. WP2

- Ask the children for other examples of pictorial and textual information they can see in the classroom or have seen outside school. WP3

Getting started whole class

- Return to the Flipover Book page and focus on the map, which shows pictorial information.

- Open the **Island** data file which shows a screen of an island surrounded by pictures.

- Ask the children to look at the pictures and say what information each picture gives. WP4

- Show the children Work Card 9 which guides them through the activity.

- The children are to make their own map of an island by choosing pictures from the screen.

- Demonstrate how to click and point a picture onto the island and move it to another place to "edit" the map.

Watchpoints ▼

WP1 The children are not expected to read the text on the Flipover Book page. This should be read to them.

WP2 This activity aims to raise awareness that information can be found all around us and it can be in different forms. You should expect the children to enter into discussion about the different types of information at a simple level. Your input should develop this understanding further. (Information can give us warnings or instructions, or can be used for entertainment or interest.)

WP3 Build upon the children's existing knowledge. Some children will be able to explore ideas in more detail than others. Try to extend the discussion by providing explanations for those children who are unable to say what the information is telling them.

WP4 You should link back to the questions asked in the introduction.

WP5 You might work with the child recording the island description, using the opportunity to extend their knowledge of the equipment and the operations performed on it such as "eject" or "rewind".

At the computer pairs

- Support each child in opening the **Island** data file and saving it to their folder as "their name + Island".

- The children should have time to talk about the pictures and to discuss their island.

- The children take it in turns to select a picture and use click and point to move it onto the island.

- The children should be encouraged to change their map by moving the pictures until they are happy with it.

- Print a copy of the island picture.

- Most children will complete a follow up task to describe their island to a partner. The partner should record the description on a tape recorder. WP5

- Extension: some children will use Resource Sheet 13 to practice using positional language.

Plenary whole class

- Use the Flipover Book page and Key Questions to discuss what the children have learned about pictorial and textual information.

- Ask individual children to show their printouts to the rest of the class. Encourage them to describe the island by using the pictorial information they can see.

- Play some of the taped descriptions to see if the children can identify the island from the information given.

- Complete the Target Sheets together.

- Explain to the children that next week they will be looking at how moving pictures give us information.

Assessment of learning outcomes ▼

- Ability to identify information (from Introduction)

- Participation in class and paired discussion

- Print out of data file (from Work Card task)

- Completed Resource Sheet

- Completed Target Sheet

Red Ted's holiday

Learning intentions

- To understand that moving pictures convey information
- To perform a simple function on ICT apparatus

Resources and setting up

- Flipover Book page 10 and Key Questions
- Resource Sheet 14 (extension only)
- Target Sheet 10 (one each)
- Work Card 10
- *Granada Writer*
- **Seaside** and **Holiday** data files
- Various holiday brochures
- A globe
- Postcards
- Passport

▼ Keywords

Lesson 4 ▶	information, video

▼ Activities

Introduction whole class

- Remind the children of last week's work where they looked at how pictures and text gave information about an island.

- Explain to the children that this week they will be looking at moving pictures.

- Use the Flipover Book page and Key Questions to introduce the idea of holidays.

- Show the children holiday brochures discussing the information found inside them. Relate these to the children's experiences of going on holiday.

- Show the children some postcards. Ask them to look at the pictures carefully and tell you something about these places. WP1

Getting started whole class

- Tell the children that the computer task requires them to find out about Red Ted's holiday by looking at four video clips.

- Open the **Seaside** data file.

- Click on the first picture.

- Tell the children they should look very carefully at each moving picture to find out as much information as possible.

- Show the children Work Card 10 focusing upon the intended outcome of the activity, that is, the children reporting back on something they have found out about where Red Ted is going on holiday.

Watchpoints ▼

WP1 Give small groups of children a number of postcards to look at from different places such as mountains, beach, city, park.

WP2 Encourage the children to look for detail by scanning each picture and discussing it in pairs. Adults should encourage the children to take the lead in discussing the pictures but they may need to use prompting questions to stimulate those children who are less willing to talk.

WP3 It should be noted that although the video clips show a seaside scene, the sea is rough and children are dressed in warm clothes. The children will need this information for the follow up task.

At the computer pairs, groups

- Support each child in opening the **Seaside** data file and saving it to their folder as "their name + Seaside".

- Using the Work Card to guide them through the activity, the children look at each video clip in turn.

- The children look at the four pictures, identifying the type of information presented and what they can find out about where Red Ted is going on holiday. WP2

- Some children will complete a follow up task to pack Red Ted's suitcase ready for his holiday using the **Holiday** data file and information they have found from the video clips. WP3

- Extension: some children will use Resource Sheet 14 to draw or write about Red Ted's holidays.

Plenary whole class

- Use the Flipover Book page and Key Questions to discuss what the children have found out about Red Ted's holiday.

- Look at some of the completed Resource Sheets, encouraging the children to talk about the information they have gathered.

- Complete the Target Sheets together.

- Use the completed Target Sheets to reinforce the new skills the children have learned.

- Explain to the children that next week they will be looking at talking books that combine pictures, text and sound.

Assessment of learning outcomes ▼

- Participation in discussion (from Introduction/Plenary)

- Ability to identify and acknowledge information in different formats (from Work Card task)

- Completed Resource Sheet

- Completed Target Sheet

UNIT 2

Talking stories

Lesson 5 ▼

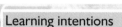

Learning intentions ▼

- To recognise how text, pictures, icons and sound are used in a computer program
- To be able to use a talking book with confidence

Resources and setting up ▼

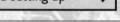

- Flipover Book page 11 and Key Questions
- Resource Sheet 15 (extension only)
- Target Sheet 11 (one each)
- Work Card 11
- Collection of different books to support introduction – recipe book, dictionary, magazine, comic
- **Story** data file
- *Granada Writer*

▼ Keywords

Lesson 5 ▶ talking book, icon, sound, picture, home, next, back, return

▼ Activities

Introduction whole class

- Remind the children of last week's work on moving pictures.

- Use the Flipover Book page and Key Questions to promote discussion about information that is presented in book form.

- Use the collection of books to support and extend the discussion. WP1

- Remind the children that information can be presented in a variety of forms, such as text, pictures and sounds.

- Explain that in this unit you will be looking at a special kind of book that has words, pictures and sounds.

Getting started whole class

- Introduce the term "talking book", showing the flashcard.

- Reinforce that talking books use words, pictures, icons and sounds to convey information.

- Open the **Story** data file (or an alternative talking book), showing the children the main menu. WP2

- Explain the use of icons.

- Demonstrate how to start the story by clicking on "Read the story".

- Tell the children they will listen to the story being read and they should think about the use of sound as well as words and pictures.

- Show the children Work Card 11 which guides them through the activity.

Watchpoints ▼

WP1 You can include more examples of different books if you wish to link with current classroom topics.

WP2 Show the children a paper-based book similar in content to the data file. An alternative talking story, such as *Nelson Thornes Sound Start Red Level CD-ROM*, could be used here. See Teacher's Support section for information on talking stories.

WP3 The children could be encouraged to predict what they think might happen next.

WP4 Explain the use of the return key.

At the computer pairs

● Support each child in opening the **Story** data file and saving it to their folder as "their name + Story".

● The children listen to the story, moving between screens using the icons and the Work Card to guide them.

● The children should be encouraged to interact with the story, joining in with the words and discussing the pictures. WP3

● Some children will use *Granada Writer* to complete a follow up task to type in words they remember from the story or use "emergent writing" to describe what happened. WP4

● Extension: some children will use Resource Sheet 15 to draw a picture about the story, discuss what might happen next in the story and type their ideas with adult support.

Plenary whole class

● Use the Flipover Book page and Key Questions to draw the children's attention to the difference between an electronic book and a paper-based one.

● Show the flashcard "talking book" and reinforce what this involves.

● Discuss the use of icons such as arrows and how they tell the computer what to do.

● Complete the Target Sheets together.

● Explain that next week the children will be looking again at all the different ways that information can be found and making a display.

Assessment of learning outcomes ▼

- Participation in whole class and group discussion (from Introduction and Plenary)
- Ability to use icons on a talking book (from Work Card task)
- Completed Resource Sheet
- Completed Target Sheet

All about...

Learning intentions ▼

- To understand that information can be presented in a variety of forms and collected from a variety of sources

- To be able to use a simple paint package or writing package

Resources and setting up ▼

- Flipover Book page 12 and Key Questions
- Target Sheet 12 (one each)
- End of Unit Target sheet (one each)
- Work Card 12
- *Granada Colours*
- *Granada Writer*
- Taped interview (optional)

▼ Keywords

Lesson 6 ▶	information, text, sound, display

▼ Activities

Introduction whole class

- Remind the children of last week's work on talking books.

- Use the Flipover Book page and Key Questions to show that information is presented in a variety of forms and collected from a variety of sources. WP1

- Show the children your prepared information book or take them through the taped interview. Discuss the information presented, focusing attention on the different sources of information. WP2

- Tell the children they are going to make a display in the classroom.

Getting started whole class

- Go back over the term "information", showing the flashcard.

- Either introduce the set topic for this unit or agree on a topic with the children.

- Discuss with the children what information they need to collect. Record this on the whiteboard.

- Discuss how they might find the information. Encourage the children to think of a wide range of sources including interviews and taking photographs, as well as books.

- Discuss with the children how they might use the computer to help them. WP3

At the computer pairs with support

- The children open *Granada Colours* or *Granada Writer*.

- The children should plan their activity prior to starting on the computer.

- The children either paint a picture or write some simple text to add information to the display.

- Some children will go on to the follow up task to produce a second picture or label.

- Printed work should be added to the display.

- Extension: some children will go on to use a camera and tape recorder to collect information, for example, the children work together in pairs to record an interview using a simple tape recorder. One child plays the part of the interviewer while the other plays the part of Red Ted or Pirate Jo.

Plenary whole class

- Use the Flipover Book page and Key Questions and the children's display to reinforce that information is all around us.

- Tell the children that they can invite their families to come and look at the display.

- Complete the Target Sheets together and allow time for the children to complete their End of Unit Target Sheets.

- Explain to the children that next week they will be moving on to a new unit on sorting.

WP1 The Internet is mentioned during this discussion. This can be omitted if not appropriate.

WP2 You should choose a topic related to your current curriculum planning. Alternatively, you could continue with the Pirates theme e.g. "Red Ted's flag", "Red Ted's treasure", "Red Ted's holiday", "About Pirate Jo" or other topics covered in this unit. Make sure there is a range of sources appropriate to the experiences of the children. There is also an option to record and play back an interview with "Pirate Jo", if you are using the "Pirates" topic. (see *Special Resources and Advanced Planning*).

WP3 Children should have had some experience of using *Granada Colours* in free play sessions to develop their mouse control (see "Watchpoints" in lesson plans, Units 1 and 2). In this lesson, therefore, the children should develop these skills by thinking about what happens when they press each of the shape icons in order to make a flag, treasure, etc. The children will need close adult support to change colours using the colour dropper and to use the fill tool or other *Granada Colours* tools. The children will develop their skills in using this simple paint package in Year 1/P2 and Year 2/P3.

Assessment of learning outcomes ▼

- Participation in whole class and group discussion (from Introduction and Plenary)

- Printouts of display contributions (from Work Card task)

- Ability to collect information (from Work Card task)

- Ability to recognise different forms of information (from Introduction)

- Completed Target Sheet

- Completed End of Unit Target Sheet

Sorting information

Overview 1

Lesson ▼ •••• **UNIT MAP**

1
- To understand that the mouse controls the pointer
- To use a mouse with a degree of hand and eye co-ordination
- To complete a simple program on the computer

2
- To understand that key pieces of information can describe objects
- To use ICT to sort information
- To manipulate objects with increasing control

3
- To understand that objects can be described using key words
- To begin to identify key words to describe objects
- To recognise and sort groups onscreen with one, two or three objects

4
- To understand that objects can be divided according to criteria
- To begin to identify the criteria that divide a set of objects

5
- To understand that objects can be identified from key words
- To find an object using given information
- To describe simple features of objects on the computer using key words

6
- To describe objects using key words
- To add labels to objects using the computer

About this unit ▼

This unit develops the children's knowledge and understanding about information. They learn that information can be used to describe objects. They sort objects using simple criteria and identify objects using key words. The children use a word list to present the information.

Lesson 1 offers some basic consolidation of the children's mouse skills, and also encourages the children to describe where objects are hidden using simple positional language. In this way, they should realise that information in general and key words in particular can give greater understanding of what objects are like and where things are.

The remainder of the unit offers the children opportunities to sort objects in different ways. The children should also be able to use some of their basic vocabulary – for example "big" and "small" and different colours, as well as prepared word lists of associated vocabulary to label objects and divide them into groups.

Integrated tasks and links

The application of the skills learned here is wide. You may wish to put them into operation in your current planning.

Mathematical development: the children will apply what they have learned in this unit when sorting shapes and objects. They will use language such as "big" and "small" to compare objects and to order them by height. They will begin to use mathematical names to describe solid and flat shapes and show curiosity and observation by talking about them or explaining why some are different. They will use developing mathematical ideas to solve problems. There are opportunities for counting objects and comparing how many there are.

Knowledge and understanding of the world: the children can apply knowledge and skills when exploring and investigating objects, identifying some features of objects they observe and looking closely for similarities and differences. They recognise patterns, shapes and colours in the world around them and can sort and categorise into simple groups.

Skills progression ▼

This unit builds upon work undertaken in Unit 1, in which the children used simple word lists to enter text onto the screen and Unit 2 where the children were looking at presenting information in different ways. The unit provides a foundation for further work on databases and assumes the children have had previous experience of sorting objects; they should also have some awareness of concepts such as big and small and have successfully completed work in previous units. The children continue to develop work in this area in Year 1/P2 Unit 4 "Labelling and classifying".

Key words

Prepare flashcards to display around the room, to remind the children during the week of the specialist vocabulary they may need. The key words can be found in the Reception/P1 Resources File and can be enlarged to A3 size on a photocopier.

Lesson 1 ▶	mouse, pointer, click, point, in, on, under, behind, in front of
Lesson 2 ▶	information, sort, point, click, corner, edge, middle
Lesson 3 ▶	information, key words, sort, match, soft, hard, smooth, big, small, smell, feel, set, drag
Lesson 4 ▶	groups, set, shape, size, sort, match, drag, key words, big, small, cube, block, sphere, ball
Lesson 5 ▶	information, key words, click, play, listen
Lesson 6 ▶	large, small, gold, blue, silver, match, click

Sorting information

Overview 2 ▼

Setting the scene ▼

1 Where's Ted?

Red Ted has lost Little Ted.
The children begin the unit by practising and consolidating their skills in using the mouse confidently and competently. Red Ted has lost his nephew, Little Ted, and the children explore the computer screen to find him and his friend by clicking and dragging furniture and objects. They also hide Little Ted and describe where they have hidden him.

2 Jigsaws

Help Red Ted complete a jigsaw.
The children develop their understanding that information helps them to solve simple jigsaw puzzles. They discuss the process of completing jigsaws using information from the pieces and the picture. The children complete jigsaws on the computer and make their own jigsaws from cards.

3 What is it?

Play Red Ted's sorting game!
The children undertake sorting activities related to the use of key words. They have to describe objects on a tray and in a feely bag/box using key words related to their senses. On the computer, the children identify and sort objects using similar key words.

Special resources and advanced planning

You will need to be familiar with the functions of the computer listed in the unit map. Spend some time each week before each lesson in familiarising yourself with those functions. You may find it useful to work through the children's Work Cards as well.

Lesson 1 ▶ Bring in a favourite teddy bear for the introduction and plenary activities. Display the flashcards around the classroom, so that the children begin to understand the technical vocabulary and positional language used in the lesson.

Lesson 2 ▶ Real jigsaws with no more than ten pieces could be used.

4 Meet Mag Pie

Help Mag Pie to tidy Red Ted's ship.
In this lesson the children develop their skills in sorting using size and shape. The children meet a new character and assist her in tidying the ship by sorting objects by size and shape. The children learn how to print work for themselves.

5 Red Ted has lost his ship

...can you help him to find it!
The children use the computer to sort objects from given information. Red Ted describes his ship and the children use the information clues to identify it from a collection of ships. The children discuss "information" and "key words" and talk about different types of information.

6 Which is which?

Sort Red Ted's treasure and label it.
In this lesson the children begin to use key words to describe objects. The key words are presented in a word list and the children select two words to describe each object on the screen. The children begin to think about criteria that are general and specific.

Lesson 3 ▶ (optional) As part of the introduction, you might collect objects similar to those used on the Flipover Book page. These would include a ball of wool, a spoon, a pair of glasses, a spiky shell, a skipping rope, a balloon, a baby's rattle and a teddy. You would need a blindfold. Alternatively, a feely bag or box of interesting objects could be used.

Lesson 4 ▶ A collection of balls and blocks of different sizes and sorting hoops are required, plus labels for the following words "big", "small", "cube", "block", "sphere", and "ball" prepared from flashcards.

Lesson 5 ▶ (optional) Examples of wood and metal and perhaps a toy ship with a mast would be useful in helping the children to visualise the key words. Ask each child to bring in a teddy from home. Tell them they will have to describe their teddy using two key words.

Lesson 6 ▶ Prepare some enlarged 50p and 5p laminated coins with words "large", "small", "silver", "gold", "blue".

Where's Ted?

Learning intentions ▼

- To understand that the mouse controls the pointer
- To use a mouse with a degree of hand and eye co-ordination
- To complete a simple program on the computer

Resources and setting up ▼

- Flipover Book page 13 and Key Questions
- Resource Sheet 16 (extension only)
- Target Sheet 13 (one each)
- Work Card 13
- **Little Ted** data file
- Teddy bear
- Objects to hide in the classroom (a hat, a book, etc.)

▼ Key words

Lesson 1 ▶	mouse, pointer, click, point, in, on, under, behind, in front of

▼ Activities

Introduction whole class

- Introduce the lesson by telling the children that you have lost your favourite teddy bear and that you want some help finding him.

- Leave the teddy bear hidden in the classroom and ask individual children to describe where the teddy bear is hiding. WP1

- Explain that Red Ted has also lost something: his nephew Little Ted.

- Use the Flipover Book page and Key Questions to develop the "story", to review the use of positional language and to set the scene for the computer task.

Getting started whole class

- Tell the children that they are going to play a game on the computer in which they have to find Little Ted and his friend in Red Ted's cabin.

- Explain that when they have found the teddies, they will put Little Ted in a different hiding place and talk to their friends about where he is hiding.

- Open the **Little Ted** data file and ask the children to describe what they can see. Explain that the activity on the computer is similar to the one on the Flipover Book page, but that on the computer they can actually move the objects to see if Little Ted is hiding. WP2

- Reinforce that the children control what happens on the screen by using the mouse to control the pointer.

Watchpoints ▼

WP1 Leave the teddy bear somewhere obvious, so that different children can describe where he is. Emphasis should be given to the use of positional language such as: "I am looking *in* my cupboard... *under* the table... *around* the classroom" etc. There are obvious links here to the children's mathematical development and to work in this area.

WP2 This activity is adapted from the *My World* activity, Find Ted. This task requires the child to increase or decrease by holding and dragging the image outwards or inwards.

WP3 An adult supporting the activity could play a guessing game with the children by giving the children instructions such as, "I think Little Ted is behind the plant", "What is behind the cupboard?" The children respond by moving the object to see if a teddy is there.

WP4 Make sure the objects are not totally hidden to make the game easier.

At the computer pairs

- Support each child in opening the **Little Ted** data file and saving it to their folder as "their name + Little Ted".

- The children take it in turns to select objects on the screen to move in order to find Little Ted and his friend.

- The children should be encouraged to discuss where Little Ted might be, using appropriate language.

- Print a copy of the screen showing where the teddies have been found.

- When both teddies have been found, some children will complete a follow up task to hide them again on the screen. This involves moving objects and placing the teddies behind them. WP3

- Extension: some children will use Resource Sheet 16 to help them place objects in specific locations.

Plenary whole class

- Use the Flipover Book page and Key Questions, together with the children's printouts, to reinforce how the computer can enable us to move pictures.

- Play a game in which you describe things you have lost and the children try to guess what it is that you have lost. Ask for a volunteer to pretend they have lost an object and get them to describe it to the class so that the other children can help them find it. WP4

- Complete the Target Sheets together.

- Explain that next week the children will use information to help them solve a puzzle.

Assessment of learning outcomes ▼

- Participation in whole class and group discussion

- Printout of completed data file (from Work Card task)

- Printout of extension task

- Ability to explain how they used the computer to complete the task

- Completed Resource Sheet

- Completed Target Sheet

Jigsaws

Lesson 2 ▼

Learning intentions ▼

- To understand that key pieces of information can describe objects
- To use ICT to sort information
- To manipulate objects with increasing control

Resources and setting up ▼

- Flipover Book page 14 and Key Questions
- Resource Sheet 17 (one per group)
- Resource Sheet 18 (extension only)
- Target Sheet 14 (one each)
- Work Card 14
- **Jigsaw** data file
- Old cards cut up to make jigsaws (optional)

▼ Key words

Lesson 2 ▶	information, sort, point, click, corner, edge, middle

▼ Activities

Introduction whole class

- Remind the children of last week's lesson where they were able to move things around the screen.

- Use the Flipover Book page and Key Questions to introduce the idea that the computer can be used to sort information by putting together a jigsaw.

- Discuss with the children their own experiences of making jigsaws at home and at school. WP1

- Show the children different jigsaws and reinforce how we use different pieces of information to complete them. WP2

- Give groups of children pieces of the jigsaw cut out from old birthday/Christmas cards (or use the picture on Resource Sheet 17) and ask them to complete the jigsaw. WP3

- Discuss how the computer might help Red Ted and the children to complete jigsaws.

Getting started whole class

- Go back to the Flipover Book page and tell the children that they are going to complete a jigsaw on the computer.

- Tell the children they must think about the different pieces of information they can see and how these help them to complete the jigsaw successfully.

- Open the **Jigsaw 1** data file, which shows a jigsaw containing 9 pieces. WP4

- Go over the task on Work Card 14 with the children, reading each instruction from the card to make sure that the children understand what they have to do.

At the computer pairs

● Support each child in opening the **Jigsaw 1** data file and saving it to their folder as "their name + Jigsaw1".

● Encourage the children to talk about what they can see on the screen, looking for information that can help them.

● Taking it in turns, the children click and point the pieces to the correct place.

● Some children will complete a follow up task to repeat the activity with one child instructing another which pieces to move.

● Extension: some children will use Resource Sheet 18 to complete **Jigsaw 2**. WP5

Plenary whole class

● Use the Flipover Book page and Key Questions together with the children's completed jigsaws, to discuss how the computer can be used to sort information. WP6

● Review the children's printouts and discuss what was hard and what was easy about the computer task. Compare their experiences with the process of putting together a normal jigsaw.

● Complete the Target Sheets together.

● Explain that next week the children will play a game to sort things into different boxes.

WP1 Discuss with the children what they find hard or easy about jigsaws, for example, are the pieces too small? Do they like doing them? With whom do they do jigsaws?

WP2 Some children are less successful in completing jigsaws because they do not know how to use information such as the completed picture to work at them systematically. You can therefore use this lesson to develop the children's thinking and reasoning skills. The computer task can also be used as an opportunity to assess the children's ability to manipulate objects with increasing control.

WP3 Cut the pictures carefully into jigsaw type pieces and muddle them up.

WP4 Differentiate according to your previous assessments of the children's ability to manipulate objects on the computer. Some children may be capable of starting with the 12-piece jigsaw on **Jigsaw 2**.

WP5 Ask another adult to work with the children on this task, prompting with the questions on the Resource Sheet.

WP6 You can put all the children's jigsaws into containers for other children to complete.

Assessment of learning outcomes ▼

● Ability to use and sort information (from Introduction and Work Card task)

● Participation in whole class and paired discussion (from Introduction and Work Card task)

● Ability to manipulate jigsaw pieces (observation from Work Card task)

● Printout of completed jigsaws (from Work Card and extension task)

● Completed Resource Sheet

● Completed Target Sheet

UNIT 3

What is it?

Lesson 3 ▼

Learning intentions ▼

- To understand that objects can be described using key words
- To begin to identify key words to describe objects
- To recognise and sort groups onscreen with one, two or three objects

Resources and setting up ▼

- Flipover Book page 15 and Key Questions
- Resource Sheet 19 (one each)
- Resource Sheet 20 (extension only)
- Target Sheet 15 (one each)
- Work Card 15
- *Granada Writer*
- **Hard and soft**, **Big and small** and **Sorting** data files
- Tray containing balloon, ball of wool, spoon, pair of glasses, spiky shell, skipping rope, baby's rattle, teddy bear (optional)

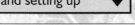

▼ Key words

| Lesson 3 ▶ | information, key words, sort, match, soft, hard, smooth, big, small, smell, feel, set, drag |

▼ Activities

Introduction whole class

- Remind the children of the previous lesson where they completed real jigsaws and jigsaws on the computer.
- Use the Flipover Book page and Key Questions to explain how key words are used to describe objects.
- Place a tray of objects, as shown on the Flipover Book page, at the front of the class to support the Flipover Book page activity.
- Show the children the flashcards for various key words that might be used to describe the objects in the tray. WP1

Getting started whole class

- Return to the Flipover Book page. Ask the children to look at each of the objects on Red Ted's tray and set them some questions to answer. WP2
- Ask further questions relating to the objects that sort them into two groups – hard, not hard, soft, not soft, smooth, not smooth. WP3
- Give each child a copy of Resource Sheet 19 and ask the children to draw a picture to match each of the key words.
- Tell the children they are going to sort some objects on the computer. They must look at the objects and the key words to help them. WP4
- Go over Work Card 15 with the children to make sure they understand what they have to do.

WP1   The tray of objects is optional, though it should help the children to identify a wider range of key words.

WP2   Questions might include: "Is it hard?" "Is it soft?" "Is it big?" "Is it small?" Point to each object in turn to get a yes/no answer. Where possible, encourage the children to set the questions themselves.

WP3   This is an important data handling activity linked to the use of Carroll Diagrams to sort a collection. Work in this area links directly to the Early Learning Goals in the area of Mathematical Development and to the *Curriculum Framework for Children 3 to 5* ("Knowledge and Understanding about the World").

WP4   Many of the activities they have used so far involve "click and point" functionality; this activity challenges the children to drag and drop the objects. You will need to demonstrate this difference for the children. Give the children plenty of opportunity to practice this new skill.

WP5   The children could use the objects in the tray to decide how to sort the objects onscreen.

At the computer pairs

● Support each child in opening the **Hard and soft** data file and saving it to their folder as "their name + Hard and soft".

● The children look at the pictures and read the key words.

● The children click and drag the pictures to the correct box. The children then add their names and print their work. WP5

● Some children will work on a follow up task to complete the **Big and small** activity. These children should then spend some time discussing how and why they have sorted the objects.

● Extension: some children will work on Resource Sheet 20, to suggest their own criterion for sorting the objects in the **Sorting** activity.

Plenary whole class

● Use the Flipover Book page and Key Questions together with the children's Resource Sheets to reinforce the use of key words to describe objects.

● Use a feely bag or box to play a game in which the children must describe what they can feel and the rest of the children have to guess what it is.

● Discuss how this game might be played on a computer and how it might differ.

● Complete the Target Sheets together.

● Explain that next week they will continue to look at how the computer can help them to sort objects into sets.

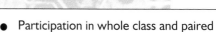

● Participation in whole class and paired discussion (from Introduction and Plenary)

● Ability to identify key words to describe objects (from Work Card task)

● Ability to sort objects on computer using own criterion (from extension task)

● Completed Resource Sheets

● Completed Target Sheet

UNIT
3

Meet Mag Pie

Lesson 4 ▼

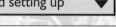

Learning intentions ▼

- To understand that objects can be divided according to criteria
- To begin to identify the criteria that divide a set of objects

Resources and setting up ▼

- Flipover Book page 16 and Key Questions
- Resource Sheet 21 (one each)
- Resource Sheet 22 (extension only)
- Target Sheet 16 (one each)
- Work Card 16
- *Granada Writer*
- **Sorting by shape**, **Sorting by size** and **Sorting by ?** data files
- Large and small balls and blocks of two different colours
- Sorting hoops
- Labels for size: "big" and "small" and shape: "block" and "ball" or "cube" and "sphere".

▼ Key words

Lesson 4 ▶ groups, set, shape, size, sort, match, drag, key words, big, small, cube, block, sphere, ball

▼ Activities

Introduction whole class

- Remind the children of last week's work on using key words to identify objects.
- Use the Flipover Book page and Key Questions to introduce sorting objects by shape or size.
- Have a collection of balls and blocks and sorting hoops. Sort the objects and ask the children to guess how you have sorted them. Repeat using different criteria. WP1
- Now ask for a volunteer to sort the objects and ask the rest of the class to guess how they have been sorted.

Getting started whole class

- Give each child a copy of Resource Sheet 21 and ask the children to complete the sheet by drawing objects from the classroom that meet each of the set criteria on the Resource Sheet. Explain that they need to identify the key words and match them to objects in the classroom. WP2
- Tell the children that they are going to help Mag Pie to tidy Red Ted's ship by sorting the toys into sets on the computer.
- Show the children Work Card 16 with the targets and task. Read through the Work Card to make sure they understand what they have to do.

Watchpoints ▼

WP1 Use labels to match children's suggestions so that you make clear the criteria by which you have sorted. Use appropriate sorting language such as "balls" and "not balls".

WP2 Emphasise the correct size language and shape names. This work has clear links to numeracy work in Reception/P1 on Measures, Shape and Space.

WP3 Encourage all of the children to describe each object in a sentence, for example: "It is small. It is a cube. It is a small cube". More confident children should be expected to use more appropriate mathematical language when describing the objects, for example "cube" rather than "block". An adult helper might be asked to work with the groups encouraging the children to explain why the object must go in the designated set.

At the computer pairs

- Support each child in opening the **Sorting by size** data file and saving it to their folder as "their name + Sorting by size".

- The children complete the task from Work Card 16 to sort the toys by size.

- Some children will use the **Sorting by shape** data file work on a follow up task to sort the toys by shape. WP3

- Extension: some children will use Resource Sheet 22 and the **Sorting by ?** data file to consider other ways of sorting the toys on the computer, for example, they can be sorted by colour ("green" and "not green").

Plenary whole class

- Use the Flipover Book page and Key Questions to review the sorting process and encourage the children to point out the key words for each set.

- Look at examples of the children's work and encourage them to reflect upon their work on the computer.

- Point out how they have sorted the objects into sets using different criteria and ask them to describe the sets in their own words.

- Ask the groups who completed the extension task to describe the other ways they found to sort the toys on the computer.

- Complete the Target Sheets together.

- Explain that next week the children will be using key words and other information to help Red Ted to find his ship!

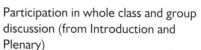

Assessment of learning outcomes ▼

- Participation in whole class and group discussion (from Introduction and Plenary)

- Printed copies of Work Card task

- Completed Resource Sheets

- Completed Target Sheet

Red Ted has lost his ship

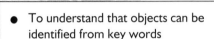

Learning intentions ▼

- To understand that objects can be identified from key words
- To find an object using given information
- To describe simple features of objects on the computer using key words

Resources and setting up ▼

- Flipover Book page and Key Questions
- Resource Sheet 23 (one each)
- Resource Sheet 24 (extension only)
- Target Sheet 17 (one each)
- Work Card 17
- **Ships** and **Flags** data files
- *Granada Writer* (extension only)
- Children's teddies

▼ Key words

| Lesson 5 ▶ | information, key words, click, play, listen |

▼ Activities

Introduction whole class

- Remind the children of last week's work on sorting objects using different criteria.
- Use the Flipover Book page and Key Questions to consolidate the children's understanding that the use of key words makes it easier to identify objects.
- Use the picture clues to establish what Red Ted's ship looks like and try to draw out key words from the children. WP1

Getting started whole class

- Give each child a copy of Resource Sheet 23 and challenge them to identify the key words related to each ship in the pictures by copying the words into the boxes beneath the pictures. WP2
- Tell the children that they are going to play a similar game on the computer so that they can help Red Ted to find his ship.
- They will hear information and decide which ship belongs to Red Ted. They need to match the ship with the information.
- Click on the **Ship** data file with the mouse. Discuss the ships on the screen. Click on the play button to listen to the information. Show the children how to click on the cross to make a ship disappear.
- Go over the rest of Work Card 17 and make sure that they are clear about what they have to do.

Watchpoints

WP1 You might have to help the children to identify some of these key words such as "mast" and "wood", as they are unlikely to have encountered them before. Write the key words on the board as the children identify them or use the flashcards. Work in this area links to sorting work in mathematics or to aspects of "Knowledge and understanding of the world" where children are encouraged to sort objects by different criteria.

WP2 You might wish to include a further activity here which links to the second computer task of finding Red Ted's flag. You would need to prepare a set of flags and some flashcards of key words for the children to identify the correct flag. You could ask the children to identify the flags by placing the key words alongside each one. If time is limited, then it might not be necessary for all children to complete both activities.

WP3 Children should be used to using a tape recorder by this stage, so this activity should help children to understand that the computer can also be used to switch sounds on and off.

WP4 You might get the children to play this game in groups and describe the objects for others to guess. With adult help, the children can type in and print out all the key words they use to describe the teddies. The children have to type their own key words in the next lesson, so this task could provide some useful consolidation.

At the computer pairs

- Support each child in opening the **Ships** data file and saving it to their folder as "their name + Ships".

- Encourage the children to discuss the ships they can see on the screen.

- The children use Work Card 17 to listen to Red Ted's information to identify his ship. WP3

- Some children will complete a follow up task to find Red Ted's flag from the **Flags** data file.

- Extension: some children will use Resource Sheet 24 and *Granada Writer* to type in descriptions of Red Ted's ship and flag using the key words they have found.

Plenary whole class

- Use the Flipover Book page and Key Questions, together with the children's printouts and Resource Sheet to review key words and the importance of giving clear information.

- Using some of the printouts, discuss the labels that match the information on the Flipover Book page.

- Ask each child to bring in a teddy. Place some of the teddies at the front of the class. Ask a child, whose teddy is on display, to describe it in two words, for example "small" and "yellow". The rest of the class try to identify the teddy. Discuss with the class why information and key words can often make it easier to identify the teddy. Discuss the features that all the teddies share and the ones that are unique to individual teddies. WP4

- Ask the pairs who completed the extension task to explain their descriptions of Red Ted's ship and flag. Why did they describe them in this way?

- Complete the Target Sheets together.

- Explain that next week the children will use their own key words to describe objects, type the key words and print them onto labels.

Assessment of learning outcomes

- Printouts of ship and flag (from Work Card task)
- Printouts of various key words and descriptions (from extension task)
- Completed Resource Sheets
- Completed Target Sheet

Which is which?

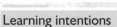

Learning intentions ▼

- To describe objects using key words
- To add labels to objects using the computer

Resources and setting up ▼

- Flipover Book page 18 and Key Questions
- Resource Sheet 25 (one each)
- Target Sheet 18 (one each)
- End of Unit Target Sheet (one each)
- Work Card 18
- **Jewels** data file
- 50p and 5p enlarged laminated coins, plus prepared labels "50p coin" and "5p coin"
- Labels for "large", "small", "blue", "silver", "gold"

▼ Key words

Lesson 6 ▶	large, small, gold, blue, silver, match, click

▼ Activities

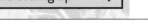

Introduction whole class

- Remind the children of last week's work on using information and key words to describe Red Ted's ship.

- Use the Flipover Book page and Key Questions to focus on labelling objects using key words. Have some labels prepared to stick onto the Flipover Book page. WP1

- Using an enlarged 50p and 5p, ask two children to come and find the correct labels to go with the two objects.

- Reinforce the idea that the object has the same name (coin) but the key words help us distinguish between the two.

Getting started whole class

- Give each child a copy of Resource Sheet 25. Challenge the children to find items in the classroom that match the key words given on the labels, then to draw these items in each of the boxes. WP2

- Using Work Card 18, tell the children that they are going to use the computer to label some of Red Ted's jewels and play his game, using key words to describe colour and size only.

- Go over the computer task with the children and make sure that they are clear about what they have to do. Look at the first jewel on the screen. Demonstrate how to click on the words so that they appear in the text box.

- Remind the children how to use a word list on the computer and to hear each pair of words spoken. WP3

WP1   You should expect the children to draw on knowledge developed in previous lessons in ICT and on work in early mathematics focused upon sorting by shape and size.

WP2   Make sure there are sufficient items around the classroom that match the criteria given on Resource Sheet 25. If not, then source appropriate items.

WP3   Word lists were covered in Unit 1. You might give some of the less confident children some of the Work Cards from this unit to practice using a word list. Some children might find this task easy while others might not yet be ready to move on to the follow up task.

WP4   The children's labels might be limited to those used in the Work Card task. However, you might extend the range of criteria to include shape, size (including comparatives such as long or longer), texture (rough and smooth) and others linked to work in other subject areas.

At the computer pairs

● Support each child in opening the **Jewels** data file and saving it to their folder as "their name + Jewels".

● Using Work Card 18, each child looks at the collection of jewels on the screen. They describe the jewel they have chosen with an adult. Encourage them to form sentences such as, "Is it blue?", "Is it big?", "Is it a round shape?"

● They then look for the appropriate words in the word list, using the speech function as additional support.

● Some children complete a follow up task to label their chosen jewel.

● Extension: some children will use *Granada Writer* and their work on Resource Sheet 25 to type their own labels to describe the objects they found in the classroom. WP4

Plenary whole class

● Use the Flipover Book page and Key Questions to establish that the children understand the use of information and key words and can describe objects on the computer using basic key words.

● Look at some of the children's printed work and discuss labelling.

● Review Resource Sheet 25 and the objects found in the classroom.

● Discuss the criteria selected for the extension task with individual children or small groups.

● Complete the Target Sheets together and allow time to complete the End of Unit Target Sheet.

● Explain that next week the children will use all the skills they have learned in a role play.

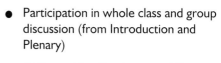

● Participation in whole class and group discussion (from Introduction and Plenary)

● Ability to identify a key word (from Work Card task)

● Print out of computer activity (from Work Card task)

● Completed Resource Sheet (including labels from extension task)

● Completed Target Sheet

● Completed End of Unit Target Sheet

Television studio

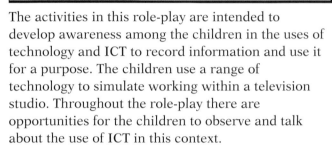

Key ICT skills ▼ • • UNIT MAP

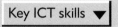

The adult will demonstrate the use of technology in order for the children:

- To become aware of technology, how it works and how we can use it in everyday life
- To find out about and identify the uses of everyday technology
- To use technology within their role-play

At the computer

- To be able to control the mouse and use left mouse clicks
- To use the mouse to select and move items on screen
- To use and understand key ICT vocabulary - for example, to follow an instruction to use the return key to move to the next line
- To understand that computers can be used to present information in a range of ways – pictures, words and sounds
- To understand how the computer can be used to change and edit text

Camera / video camera

- To understand that a digital camera is different from a still camera
- To understand that a video camera records movement and sequences of images
- To operate a camera to take photographs, thinking about the images taken
- To review photographs and think about ways to improve images

Tape recorder

- To use a tape recorder to record and play back information

Other key skills

- Refer to Links Chart on pages 104–106

About this role-play ▼

The activities in this role-play are intended to develop awareness among the children in the uses of technology and ICT to record information and use it for a purpose. The children use a range of technology to simulate working within a television studio. Throughout the role-play there are opportunities for the children to observe and talk about the use of ICT in this context.

Organisation ▼

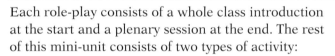

Each role-play consists of a whole class introduction at the start and a plenary session at the end. The rest of this mini-unit consists of two types of activity:

Adult-led activities, which are planned and supported by an adult in either a teaching role or as a "play partner" to develop the children's skills in the use of technology to support their play, for example, supporting the children in using a video recorder to video a role-play news programme.

Child-initiated learning, in which the children use the television studio for their own purposes. These activities include the use of technology and "pretend" technology and offer valuable evidence of the children's ability to transfer learning from the adult-led activities to their play. See *Special Resources and advanced planning* section.

Each role-play is intended to last for half a term – about five to six weeks – depending on the extent to which you wish to develop the activities suggested.

Integrated tasks and links ▼

1 Communication, language and literacy

This unit offers opportunities for the children to engage in different aspects of communication, language and literacy. They participate in "speaking and listening" activities, which develop their confidence and ability to communicate. The children use their imagination and knowledge to extend their use of language in a new context, thus increasing an understanding of the role and use of language. They begin to create simple pieces of writing and are encouraged to express their own ideas by writing on the computer. The children should also be encouraged to question why things happen and offer simple explanations as they use new software.

2 Knowledge and understanding of the world

The children develop a greater understanding of something they take for granted at home and school, the development of television programmes. By investigating how television works, they extend their knowledge of different jobs as well as learning how to operate a range of simple equipment. They also begin to understand why things happen and how things work. As they become aware of the different types of technology available, the children's interest in ICT should increase. There are links with weather studies, encouraging the children to observe, find out about the natural world and investigate their environment.

3 Personal, social and emotional development

This unit is based on collaborative play in which roles and jobs are negotiated. The children need to work together and coordinate their play. This will help them develop skills in turn taking and compromising. Confidence levels increase as the children become more familiar with the roles they are playing. The viewing of their own recorded performances will increase the children's self-esteem and ability to talk in larger group situations. The context will enable the children to demonstrate increasing independence in selecting and carrying out activities through self-motivation. They will develop their awareness of the behavioural expectations within the television studio and in the operation of particular ICT equipment.

4 Physical development

The children will use a range of different equipment and will develop their gross and fine motor skills, for example, using cameras or acting as presenters. They will develop their understanding that equipment has to be used safely and that items are costly to replace. There are also links with movement as the children move with confidence and imagination in a safe environment.

5 Creative development

The unit encourages the children to use their imagination by means of a variety of media to express their ideas, for example, creating simple tunes for news programmes, creating pictures using a paint package to display as backdrops to stories, creating props for art shows.

Key words ▼

Prepare the flashcards to display around the room, to remind the children, during the week, of the specialist vocabulary they may need. The Key words can be found in the Reception/P1 Resources File and can be enlarged to A3 size on a photocopier.

television, camera, video, recording, tape recorder, studio, action, weather forecast

camera operator, newsreader, weather forecaster

control, buttons, return, click, icon, mouse, rewind, playback

Television studio

Overview 2 ▼

I **Reporting the weather**	The children investigate weather forecasts from the television to support their understanding of how technology is used to present information. They discuss the uses of animation and different background screens to present weather information that is changing over time. The children learn about the uses of control technology to make changes on screen. They create and present their own weather forecasts to show weather changes over a two-day period, developing their skills of prediction.
2 **Interviewing people**	The children use a tape recorder to interview different people on a selected subject to link in with other curriculum topics, for example, the building of new houses nearby, concerns about a busy road, about their pets. The children will have used a tape recorder in Unit 2. Here, they develop its use by linking it to other technologies in Activity 3. The children also develop their skills in talking and posing questions. The interviews will be used again in Activity 5.
3 **Using cameras**	This activity links with Activity 2. The children use a digital and still camera to take a photograph of the person they have just interviewed. The children are encouraged to review the images they have taken, thinking about how the images could be improved. Digital images are downloaded onto the computer (see Teacher's Support section for help with this). The images are then used in Activity 5.
4 **And here is the news…**	The children "create" a piece of news and are supported in the writing process through the use of a word processing package. The children role-play presenting the news to a group in front of a pretend camera.
5 **Filming the programme: Take I**	The main focus of this activity is to use a video camera to record the children's role-play in the television studio. The children are encouraged to develop their skills in using the video camera, though an alternative activity is also suggested in which the children take on the role of the director and tell the adult what to film. The children use materials from the other activities to draw the unit to a close.

Special resources and advanced planning

The children will learn more about a role-play context if they are actively involved in the process of setting up the role-play area. The whole class introduction should focus the children's attention on what a television studio might look like. It is from this starting point that the children decide what should go into the studio and how it should be organised. You might also place information books about television in the book corner.

To add to the introduction of the television studio context, you might check whether any local colleges or universities offering media courses would agree to a visit from your class.

Alternatively, you might contact a local television studio if you have one in your area. The studio would be able to offer experience of the "blue screen", which is difficult to emulate in school.

Resources for both adult-led and child-initiated learning are needed as follows:

Children initiated activities

Television screen made from a big cardboard box	Writing materials for creating reports
Television camera made from junk	Toy cameras
Microphones	Computer
Desk for presenting	Tape recorder and tapes

Adult-led activities

Introduction
A television and video player are required. You should prepare a video containing short excerpts from a range of programmes. These should include a news programme, a current affairs programme for children such as Blue Peter, a children's game show and a wildlife or nature programme.

Activity 1
A computer with a CD-ROM drive and printer, a television and video player are required. You should pre-record a video of a complete weather forecast ready for the activity. It would also be helpful to prepare a set of word and phrase flashcards related to the weather, such as "high winds", "rain from the west", "sunshine and showers", "sunny intervals", "gales", "sleet and snow". Finally, copy and cut out sets of weather symbols from Resource Sheet 11. Attach Blu-Tack™ to the back of each symbol.

Activity 2
You will need a cassette recorder and a supply of blank audio-cassettes with labels for this activity. Arrange for some "key people" to be interviewed by the children. Depending upon the focus of the interview, identify people within and/or visitors to the school.

Activity 3
You will need a digital and a still camera for this activity (see Teacher's Support section for information on digital cameras). You should ask the people interviewed in Activity 2, above, if they mind having their pictures taken. If using a digital camera, you will need access to the appropriate computer imaging software. If possible, you should get this installed on a standalone computer in the classroom or identify which computer already has the software installed. For still pictures, you should use a polaroid or instamatic camera, where the picture is processed straight away, or you will need to allow time for the film to be developed.

Activity 4
A classroom computer with a word processing package such as Granada Writer will be required for this activity. The computer should have a printer attached to it.

Activity 5
This activity brings together all the other activities. The children will video a complete "programme" consisting of a weather forecast, an interview to accompany a photograph and a short news report. Prior to the recording, ensure that the photographs taken in Activity 3 appear on the computer screen or are pinned to a board ready for the accompanying interview. Also, set up the weather maps from Activity 1. A television and video player will be required to play back the completed programme.

Television studio

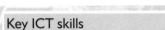

Key ICT skills ▼

The adult will demonstrate the use of technology in order for the children:

● To become aware of technology, how it works and how we can use it in everyday life

● To find out about and identify the uses of everyday technology

● To use technology within their role-play

(For other ICT learning intentions, see Unit Overview, page 50.)

Resources and setting up ▼

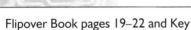

● Flipover Book pages 19–22 and Key Questions
● Resource sheets 11 and 26
● Work Card 7
● *Granada Writer*
● **Weather** data file from Unit 2 lesson 1
● See *Special resources and advanced planning* page 53 for individual activities.

▼ Activities

Introduction whole class

● Ask the children what sort of programmes they watch on the television. Make a list on the board to show the variety and organise the programmes into groups such as cartoons, information, serials, quizzes and news. Talk about the different types of programmes.

● Use the Flipover Book page 19 and Key Questions 1 to develop the children's knowledge about how television programmes are made and what a television studio looks like, with particular focus on the news. WP1

● Match the flashcards (see page 51) to the objects in the picture.

● Show a video containing excerpts from a range of different types of programmes. While watching the video, identify those programmes that are made in a studio and focus attention on the way the studio is arranged. WP2

Getting started whole class

● Discuss with the children how they might set up their television studio to make a news programme. (See *Special resources and advanced planning* page 53.)

● Challenge the children to think of an appropriate name for the studio, e.g. Class television.

● How big will it be? Mark out in the classroom the boundaries for the role-play area. What do we need to put inside it? Make a list of play equipment, organising groups of children to make props.

● What roles will the children take? Camera operator, newsreader, weather forecaster, lighting coordinator and so on. WP3

● Create the television studio role-play area. (See *Special resources and advanced planning* page 53.)

▼ Main activities

1 Reporting the weather
groups

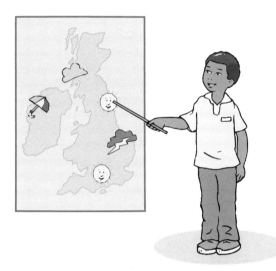

- The key skills behind this activity have already been covered in Unit 2, Lesson 1. Here, the children create two weather maps to show how the weather changes over a period of time. Please read over Unit 2, Lesson 1 again prior to undertaking this activity.

- Show the children a video of a complete weather forecast. If possible, use one taken from a children's television programme. Focus on how the report shows the weather changing over a period of time and the language used by the weather forecaster. Note also the animations on the screen. Tell the children how the weather forecaster controls the changing screen using technology – a button linked to a computer rather like a mouse.

- Display sample sentences and key words to act as prompts for the children to help them develop appropriate language. WP4

- Use the Flipover Book page 20 and Key Questions 2 to develop children's language and presentation skills.

- Using the weather symbols from Resource Sheet 11, model a forecast using appropriate actions. Discuss the difference between using computer animations to display information and demonstrating this information by hand.

- Open the **Weather** data file from Unit 2 Lesson 1. Remind the children that they have used this data file before and demonstrate the click and point technique for moving pictures.

- Tell the children that they are going to make two weather maps, one for today's weather and one to show what the weather might be like tomorrow. The Work Card from Unit 2, Lesson 1 will help them with this. Tell the children they will have to guess what the weather is like in different parts of the country and predict what they think will happen tomorrow. Explain that they will have to present this information, which will be filmed (see Activity 5).

- Extension: show the children weather pictures printed in newspapers to help some children develop their presentations further.

- When the maps have been produced, each child should present their weather forecast to the group. Emphasis should be placed upon using both actions and language. Encourage the children to review what they have done and to comment on each other's performances.

 The children could use the Flipover Book page or computer during their own role-play.

2 Interviewing people
pairs

- Use the Flipover Book page 21 and Key Questions 3 to introduce the role of technology in presenting people's opinions.

- Tell the children that they are going to interview someone. They will work as a pair, one being the interviewer and one operating the equipment. While two are interviewing, the rest of the group will watch and learn.

- Decide on the focus for the interview and discuss what questions they might ask. WP5

- Extension: some children may be able to formulate more probing questions.

- Play back the interviews and encourage the children to review what they have done. WP6

 Children can use the tape recorder to interview each other as part of their role-play.

 3 Using cameras
pairs

- This activity links with Activity 2. The children use a camera to take a photograph of the person they have interviewed.

- Use the Flipover Book page 22 Key Questions 4 to introduce the children to different types of cameras.

- Tell the children that they are going to use the digital and the still camera for this activity. They are going to take a picture of the person they interviewed using both cameras. WP7

- Discuss key issues when taking a photograph, i.e. looking through the view finder, holding the camera still and level, deciding whether to take landscape or portrait images, keeping the image in the centre of the picture.

- Let the children decide where they want to take the photo – *in situ* or in the 'studio'.

- Use the digital camera to review images recorded and show the children how these can be erased if they are not happy with them. Compare the digital and still cameras. (See Teacher's Support section.)

- Work with the children to download the images on to the computer.

- Review both sets of photos when available. (See *Special resources and advanced planning* page 53.)

 Children can use play cameras to take photographs of people to use in their role-play.

▼ Main activities

4 And here is the news...
groups

- Use the Flipover Book page 19 to focus on the role of the newsreader and tell the children that they are going to write a news story to present in the television studio and that this story will be filmed.

- Open *Granada Writer* and type in the words "The News" explaining what this means. Decide on the focus for the news: this could relate to the Big Book of the week or, for example, a lost dog or "the visit".

- Depending upon skill levels, differentiate the activity by entering the text onto the computer for the children as they discuss their ideas or setting up a word list with key words which the children can use to make simple sentences.

- Support the children in creating the piece of text. Edit and refine as necessary.

- Taking turns to play different roles, children present their news stories, while being recorded using a pretend video camera. This will give children opportunities to practise and rehearse their speaking and presentation skills. Encourage the children to talk to the camera. The rest of the group should watch and reflect upon their performances.

- Extension: allow children to write the story for themselves using "emergent writing"; you (or another adult) could make notes on the printout to remind the children of the text and its meaning. WP8

Children can choose to "write" news bulletins using "emergent writing" on the computer and/or read the news in their role-play.

5 Filming the programme: Take 1
whole class

- Use the Flipover Book page 19 to focus the children's attention on the control panels in the editing suite. Explain how these enable the news to move from one image to another – for example, showing the newsreader, then cutting to the weather forecaster, then cutting to a piece of film or an interview.

- Tell the children that they are going to make a news programme using a video camera. Explain that the cameras used in actual television programmes would be better than the video camera. WP9

- Explain that the programme will consist of a short news bulletin, an interview to accompany a picture and a weather forecast.

- On the board, write a schedule for the programme running order and who is taking which role.

Continued

▼ Main activities

- Show the children how to use the video camera. Recap on the skills needed when using the camera. Introduce, if appropriate, zoom in and zoom out buttons. Make sure the children understand that the picture is moving and that movement of the camera will change the focus of the image. Allow the children to practise using the video camera, with close support, in the television studio.

- Set up the **Weather** data file on the computer and prepare the photographs and tapes.

- *Take 1*: Make sure the children are prepared in their roles: newsreader, weather forecaster and interviewer.

- Film the entire programme. Play back and review. Discuss aspects for improvement.

- *Take 2*: Repeat with different children in role.

- Extension: some children will use Resource Sheet 26 to design their own television studio for a programme of their choice. Encourage the children to annotate using the flashcards for the unit.

 Children can use the pretend camera to film each other during their own role-play.

▼ Activities

Plenary

- Use the Flipover Book page 19 and Key Questions 1 to review what the children have learned about the different types of technology used within this setting.

- Recap on each activity showing examples if possible of work undertaken.

- Play again one of the final news programmes and encourage the children to reflect upon the process of using technology – what was difficult, what was easy, and why?

- Discuss what changes they would need to make to the studio if it were to be used to film an art programme.

Follow up work

- If possible undertake changes suggested in the Plenary and allow the children the opportunity to rehearse art activities before another "filming".

- Play the video in your assembly to demonstrate to the rest of the school what your class has achieved.

- Take photos to record the role-play area for your next parents' evening and for assessment purposes.

- Make a class big book to record events/activities for this unit.

Watchpoints ▼

WP1 It is unlikely that children will know much about how the technology works. Explain to them the use of blue screens to project images and the weather person's use of the control to change background pictures. (See Introduction page v)

WP2 This is optional but can provide children with clear images of the different types of programmes – ones that are made in studios and those that are made on location.

WP3 You will need to play alongside the children to support them in fulfilling their chosen roles.

WP4 The children may not be able to read these phrases but they can act as a reminder for any adult playing alongside the children.

WP5 Think about keeping notes to remind you and the children about the points discussed and to act as prompts. As an extension the children could read the questions.

WP6 Ask the children to think about speaking clearly and audibly, the use of intonation, the confidence and awareness of the interviewee by their use of conventions such as "please" and "thank you". Keep a list of who worked together and the interviewees for Activity 3.

WP7 If the school does not possess a digital camera you might try to borrow one from the LEA. (See Teacher's Support section.)

WP8 For the extension task, you might also allow children to elaborate their news story by adding further information, that is, to *ad lib*.

WP9 Children will need time to practise the skill of "filming" using a video camera. This is a valuable experience and the different "takes"' will reflect the developing skills. You may wish to let the children "play" with the camera prior to filming to get used to the controls. Alternatively, the children could simply act as "directors" telling you, the "cameraman", where to point the camera.

Assessment of learning outcomes ▼

Activity I
- Printouts of weather forecasts (from Work Card task)
- Ability to present information using animated software

Activity 2
- Ability to operate a tape recorder
- Ability to review the recording made

Activity 3
- Ability to operate a camera
- Images taken using cameras

Activity 4
- Understanding that the computer can create "news" that can be changed and edited
- Confidence in presenting to the camera

Activity 5
- Ability to use a video
- Awareness of technology, how it works and how we can use it in everyday life

Space: star ship

Overview 1 ▼

UNIT MAP

Key ICT skills ▼

The adult will model the use of technology in order for the children:

- To become aware of technology, how it works and how we can use it in everyday life
- To find out about and identify the uses of everyday technology
- To use technology within their role-play

At the computer

- To understand that computers can be used to present information in a range of ways – pictures, words and sounds
- To input simple words and numbers using the keyboard and word list
- To use a paint package with increasing confidence and control to include detail within their picture
- To begin to use simple control devices

Camera/digital camera

- To understand that a digital camera is different from a still camera
- To operate a camera to take photographs, thinking about the images taken
- To review photographs and think about ways to improve images

Tape recorder

- To use a tape recorder to record and play back information
- To evaluate the completed tape recording

Programmable toys

- To begin to understand how to program a programmable toy using CM to clear memory and arrow keys to determine direction

Other key skills

- Refer to Links Chart on page 104–106

About this role-play ▼

This "fantasy play" will develop awareness in the uses of technology and information and communication technology to record and use information for a purpose within a fantasy situation. The children will use a range of technology to simulate working on a star ship. They develop and extend their skills in technology use by using familiar programs, for example, a paint package, in a more sophisticated way. Throughout the role-play there are opportunities for the children to observe and talk about the use of ICT in this context.

Organisation ▼

Each role-play consists of a whole class introduction at the start and a plenary session at the end. The rest of this mini-unit consists of two types of activity.

Adult-led activities, which are planned and supported by an adult in either a teaching role or as a "play partner" to develop the children's skills in the use of technology to support their play, for example, supporting the children in using a tape recorder to record a "Captain's Log".

Child-initiated learning, in which the children use the star ship for their own purposes. These activities include the use of technology and "pretend" technology and offer valuable evidence of the children's ability to transfer learning from the adult-led activities into their play. See *Special resources and advanced planning* page 63.

Each role-play is intended to last for half a term – about five to six weeks – depending on the extent to which you wish to develop the activities suggested.

Integrated tasks and links ▼

1 Communication, language and literacy

This unit offers tremendous opportunities for the children to engage in different aspects of communication, language and literacy. The children will interact with others, negotiating roles and activities. They will be involved in speaking and listening activities, developing their confidence and ability to communicate as "speakers". Using a tape recorder the children begin to organise, sequence and clarify their thinking. The children use their imagination and knowledge within a fantasy situation to increase their understanding of the role and in so doing, extend their use of language and develop new vocabulary.

2 Mathematical development

The children create their own alien using a simple computer program. They are challenged to count the number of eyes, ears, noses, mouths and spots on their alien. They also use language such as bigger or smaller, more or less to compare the different aliens. The children create simple pictograms to display different ways of sorting and classifying the aliens.

3 Knowledge and understanding of the world

The children become involved in building and constructing objects to support their role-play within the star ship. They talk about, observe and find out information about the natural world and beyond. They begin to think about what this place is like to live in and what other planets would be like as environments. The children continue to develop their understanding of technology and the way it impacts upon their learning and on the real world. They use programmable toys to begin to engage with control and modelling.

4 Personal, social and emotional development

This unit is based on collaborative play in which roles and jobs are negotiated. The children need to work together and coordinate their play. This develops skills in turn taking and compromising. Confidence levels should increase as the children become more familiar with the roles they are playing. The context will enable the children to demonstrate increasing independence in selecting and carrying out activities through self-motivation. They are also encouraged to evaluate their own "captain's log" which increases the children's self esteem and ability to talk in larger group situations.

5 Physical development

The children use a range of different equipment and develop their gross and fine motor skills, for example, in using cameras and refining mouse control. They develop their understanding that equipment has to be used safely and that items are costly to replace. There are also links with movement as the children move with confidence and imagination in a safe environment.

6 Creative development

This unit encourages children to develop their imagination in a fantasy situation with links to characters drawn from fiction, television or video stories with which they might be familiar. The children use their imagination in a variety of media to express their ideas, for example, creating pictures using a paint package to create "props" for the star ship.

Key words ▼

Prepare the flashcards to display around the room, to remind the children, during the week, of the specialist vocabulary they may need. The key words can be found in the Reception/P1 Resources File and can be enlarged to A3 size on a photocopier.

control, print, record, replay, icon, camera

ID, log, grid

Role-play
2

Overview 2 ▼

Space: star ship

Setting the scene ▼

1 **Meet the crew**	The children use a digital or still camera to take a photograph for their Space ID card. The photographs are inserted into a pro-forma, designed in *Granada Writer*. Using a word list and/or the keyboard the children enter details about their space ID such as name ("Captain Zorg"), age and what planet they are from. The children use these ID cards when working in the role-play area.
2 **Which alien?**	This activity has a mathematical focus. The children create another alien face using prepared features on a computer screen. They choose a starting shape for a face and add eyes, noses, ears, mouths and spots. The children choose the number of each feature they wish to put on their alien. The resulting aliens are used to create simple pictograms and to generate counting activities. The children are encouraged to pose their own questions to analyse the information.
3 **Aliens**	Using *Granada Colours*, the children create a picture of an alien from another planet. The children are encouraged to add detail to their image by using smaller shapes or the pen icon, such as adding eyes, mouth and nose.
4 **Captain's log**	The children use a tape recorder to record a "Captain's Log" of their adventures in space. The children are encouraged to think about events that have taken place, the order in which these have happened and the type of information that might be recorded, such as new planets visited rather than what time they went to bed. The children are encouraged to review their log and think about ways to improve the information.
5 **Dress the alien**	The children use a programmable toy (Pixie, Pip or Roamer) to begin to understand control. The programmable toy is dressed up as an alien. The children navigate the "alien" around a simple space obstacle course using arrow keys for forward, backward, right turn and left turn.
6 **To the planet**	This activity builds upon Activity 5 in developing the children's knowledge of control technology. On the computer, the children use arrow icons to navigate the star ship across a grid on the screen to reach the planet Mars. Directions of forwards, backwards, turn right and turn left are central to controlling the star ship.

Special resources and advanced planning

The children will learn more about a role-play context if they are actively involved in the process of setting up the role-play area. The whole class introduction should focus the children's attention on imagining what it would be like on a star ship using their knowledge of characters drawn from fiction, television or video.

From this discussion, make a list of requirements for creating a star ship in the classroom. The children could draw plans of what it might actually look like. The construction of the star ship might involve the following items:

Children-initiated activities

An assortment of different-sized empty boxes to make the props
Bottle tops, buttons and discs to make the control panels
Black sugar paper to create a cone for the nose of the star ship
Tape recorder

Create a "window" onto which the children can paint planets and stars
Spray-painted wellington boots and silver and other fabric to make simple costumes of "aliens" created by the children
Information books about space in the book corner

Adult-led activities

Introduction
Prepare labels for "space", "planet", "Mars", "controls", "stars" and spread them around the classroom attaching them using Blu-Tack™.

Activity 1
You will need a digital or still camera for this activity. If using a digital camera, you will need access to the appropriate computer imaging software. If using a still camera, you will need to allow time for the film to be processed. Prepare the **Crew** data file.

Activity 2
A computer with a CD-ROM drive and a printer are required. Resource Sheet 27 is needed for the extension activity.

Activity 3
A classroom computer with a paint package (such as *Granada Colours*) and a printer is required for this activity. Resource Sheet 28 is needed for the extension task.

Activity 4
You will need a cassette recorder and a supply of blank audio-cassettes with labels for this activity. A built-in or plug-in microphone is required. The children will need to use the information on their ID from Activity 1.

Activity 5
A programmable toy, such as Pixie, Pip or Roamer is required here. (Roamer is used to demonstrate in the Work Cards and Teacher's Support section).
A collection of fabrics and odds and ends such as feathers, pipe cleaners, beads are needed to "dress" the programmable toy as an alien. To create a space environment use PE cones with attached pictures of a comet, a shooting star and the Moon. Use a globe or blue ball to represent Earth.

Activity 6
A computer with a CD-ROM drive is needed. Cut out and laminate the arrows on Resource Sheet 29, and the space features on Resource Sheet 30. Have a supply of Blu-Tack™ available to stick these to the Flipover Book page.

Space: star ship

Key ICT skills ▼

The adult will model the use of technology in order for the children:

● To become aware of technology, how it works and how we can use it in everyday life

● To find out about and identify the uses of everyday technology

● To use technology within their role-play

Resources and setting up ▼

● Flipover Book pages 23–24 and Key Questions
● Resource Sheets 27–30
● Work Cards 19–21
● *Granada Writer*
● *Granada Colours*
● **Crew** data file
(See *Special Resources and advanced planning* page 63 for individual activites.)

▼ Activities

Introduction whole class

● Use the Flipover Book page 23 and Key Questions 1 to find out about the children's knowledge of space and science fiction and to develop the children's ideas about flying in space and working in a star ship.

● Ask if any of the children have watched television programmes or read books about space travel.

● Show the children information books about space.

● Match the flashcards to the objects in the picture, ensuring that all of the children have some understanding of the layout of a star ship.

Getting started whole class

● Discuss with the children the setting up of their star ship. Decide what it will be called. Think of an appropriate name and write this on the Flipover Book page.

● How big will the star ship be? Mark out in the classroom the boundaries for the role-play area. What do we need to put inside? Make a list of play equipment and get the children to make props.

● What roles will the children take? Discuss all the possible options such as captain, doctor, engineer, navigator, pilot and explain a little about the requirements of each role.

● Create the role-play area. (See *Special Resources and advanced planning* page 63.)

▼ Main activities

1 All aboard: meet the crew
pairs/groups

- In this activity the children make a personal identity card, which they use when taking the role of a crew member on the star ship.

- The children open the **Crew** data file. Each child enters their space name and age, and the planet they are from. Encourage the children to make up a new name when on the star ship such as Captain Zorg, K45, Dr Orion.

- The children should add a photograph to their identity cards. Three options are available here:

   Use a digital camera to take a photograph of each child, which is then downloaded into the *Granada Writer* data file. WP1

   Use a still camera to take a photograph of each child, which is then scanned into the computer and inserted into the *Granada Writer* data file.

   Use a still camera to take individual photographs, which are then glued onto the identity card when it has been completed and printed out.

The identity cards are then printed and placed in a folder entitled "Crew", which is kept on the star ship.

 The children place their ID cards on the outside of the star ship when they are playing inside. They could use the sheets to engage in emergent writing activities during their play to record space journeys, etc.

2 Which alien?
pairs

- Go through the instructions on Work Card 19 with the children, reading each instruction to make sure that all of the children understand the computer task.

- Using the **Alien** data file, the children create their own alien face using prepared face outlines to which they can add eyes, ears, noses, mouths, antennae and spots. The children choose how many of each they wish to place on their picture and should be encouraged to talk with their partners about their alien as they are creating it. WP2

- The children should be encouraged to count how many of each feature they have selected. The children also enter a name for their alien. WP3

- Extension: some children will complete an extension task to type in the number of eyes, noses, spots they have put on their alien. Resource Sheet 27 encourages the children think about their alien in more detail.

 The children could prepare more aliens on their own using the **Aliens** data file, when they are familiar with the Work Card instructions.

▼ Main activities

3 Aliens
pairs

- Open *Granada Colours*.

- Go through the instructions on Work Card 20 with the children, reading each instruction to make sure that they all understand the computer task.

- Using Work Card 20, the children create a picture of an alien from another planet. Encourage the children to use basic shapes to start off with and to fill them using the floodfill tool. WP4

- Extension: some children will use Resource Sheet 28 to complete an extension task to add more detail to their picture and add a name for their alien and the planet from which it comes using the text tool. WP5

 Place a box of oddments, including fabrics, in the role-play area. The children could use the materials in the box to dress as aliens.

4 Captain's log
pairs

- Explain that the captain of the ship has to record what happens each day and this is called a "log". Tell the children that they are going to make their own log to describe an adventure they have had in space. WP6

- Give the children thinking time as to what they might say using ID cards from Activity 1 to give prompts. Use the Flipover Book page 23 and their pictures of aliens from Activity 2 to stimulate ideas.

- Use the children's experiences of watching any space programmes on television, such as black holes, attacks by other space ships, meteor showers, etc.

- Tape record the children's log either as an individual activity or a combined group response. Replay, evaluate and suggest improvements.

 The children could use blank tapes and a tape recorder to record the captain's log during their own play.

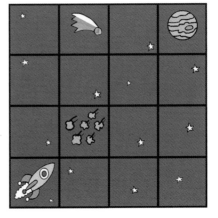

▼ Main activities

5 Dress the alien
groups

- Show the children the programmable toy and tell them that this is an alien who is coming to visit Earth.

- Let the children dress the alien with resources available.

- As the crew of the star ship, the children have to give the alien directions from their home planet to Earth.

- Go through Work Card 21 with the children and demonstrate how the programmable toy works. Give the children opportunities to explore and experiment with the arrow keys. WP7

- Place a blue ball on the carpet away from the "alien" and discuss what movements the "alien" would need to make to get to "Earth". Program the "alien" and review what happened by questioning the crew, e.g. *Did the "alien" travel far enough? How far does he still have to go?*

- Return the "alien" to the starting position and try again. Move the "Earth" to different positions to change the length of the journey. Next introduce movement of the "alien" through angles. (See Teacher's Support section.)

- Extension: some children may complete an extension task to add more features to the space scene, such as a comet or shooting stars which the alien has to move around.

 The children can free play with the "alien" to practise and explore simple control technology.

6 To the planet
whole class, then pairs

- Remind the children of how they programmed the alien in Activity 5 to control its movements.

- Use the Flipover Book page 24, prepared Resource Sheets 29 and 30 and Key Questions 2 to extend simple ideas about control and modelling on the computer.

- Explain that they will be taking the role of pilot of the star ship and they will be travelling to the planet Mars.

- Go through Work Card 22 with the children, reading each instruction from the card to make sure that they understand what they have to do.

- Demonstrate the use of the arrows to move forward, backwards and turn left and right. WP8

- On the computer open the **Planets** data file.

- The children use the Work Card instructions to move the star ship to Mars on the computer using the arrow icons. WP9

▼ Activities

Plenary

- Use the Flipover Book page 23 and Key Questions 1 to review the key ICT skills developed through the activities.

- Recap on each activity showing examples of the children's work. Focus upon how the technology supported the learning. Ask the children to explain their work and reflect on what was hard and what was easy and why.

- Complete the Target Sheets together.

- Take a photograph of the children with the star ship. Dismantle the star ship and place the folder entitled "Crew" into the book corner for children to review.

Follow up work

- Cover the sand tray with silver foil. In small world play, get the children to make miniature space buggies and use these to develop positional and directional language to extend their skills in programming and giving instructions.

- Make space music using a variety of instruments and record on a tape recorder to be played during tidy-up time.

- Play a space music CD and think about ways of moving to the music.

- Take a photograph of the crew as a reminder of this unit and use this in a display or even send it to the local newspaper.

- Make a class big book to record events/activities from this unit.

Watchpoints ▼

WP1 Let the children take the photographs of each other if possible.

WP2 The red outline for the face that appears when the data file is opened is one of the three options. The green and blue shapes on the bottom left of the screen can also be selected.

WP3 The printed alien pictures can be used to create simple pictograms relating to the shape and colour of the face, the number of eyes, mouths etc. Encourage counting by asking questions such as: *How many aliens have more than one head? How many have no spots? More than 10 spots?* Encourage children to pose questions themselves. Prompt them to think about the information they have input.

WP4 The children were introduced to the *Granada Colours* program in Unit 2, using the shape tools to make a flag for Red Ted's ship. Work Card 20 extends their knowledge of this program to include the use of these tools to add closer detail. This activity should include close adult support as it involves mouse control and manipulation skills that may be beyond some less confident children. Work in this area is consolidated in *Nelson Thornes Primary ICT Year 1/P2*.

Be particularly careful to explain the use of the Undo tool.

WP5 The name of the alien can be added by an adult for children who are less confident in using the keyboard. Give support for unusual names the children may think of such as "Narg".

WP6 You could prepare an example to play to the children. Include information such as name, planet, times, things seen etc. Select the children to play the part of the captain who have the confidence to speak in groups and interact with others. They should also be able to organise, sequence and clarify their thinking to make up stories. Differentiate the activity and select groups accordingly. Other members of the

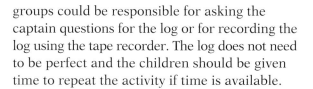

Watchpoints ▼

groups could be responsible for asking the captain questions for the log or for recording the log using the tape recorder. The log does not need to be perfect and the children should be given time to repeat the activity if time is available.

WP7 If this is the first time any of the children have used a programmable toy, spend some time familiarising them with the control keys. Many children will need extensive support with this activity. Initially, you may have to do most of the programing yourself. If any of the children have used a programmable toy before, ask them to explain how it works. These children could then play the role of "navigator". The navigators could show the other crew members how to work the controls, what the arrow keys mean, etc. The Teacher's Support section shows the basic commands for controlling the Roamer.

WP8 Turning left and right will be particularly difficult for children to master at this age. You will probably need to demonstrate how this works but, in most cases, not expect them to be able to program the toy themselves.

WP9 Some children may need adult support here, although trial and error strategies are useful ways for the children to explore controlling movements on the screen. The children act out the movements to reinforce forwards, backwards, left and right. Please note: the instructions on Work Card 22 cause the star ship to crash. Allow plenty of time for the children to discuss in groups how they might program the star ship to reach Mars.

Assessment of learning outcomes ▼

Activity 1
- Printout of ID
- Ability to use a camera to take a photograph

Activity 2
- Printout of alien (from Work Card task)
- Ability to describe alien by identifying the number of features

Activity 3
- Printout of alien painting (from Work Card task)
- Ability to use shapes or the pen tool to add detail to picture

Activity 4
- Ability to operate a tape recorder
- Confidence in talking

Activity 5
- Ability to move the alien (from the Work Card task)
- Ability to control the alien in order to move from A to B

Activity 6
- Ability to control the star ship using arrow keys (from Work Card task)
- Ability to predict outcomes of movement

Red Ted's ship

Key Questions 1 ▼

Introduction

- This is Red Ted. Red Ted is a pirate. He lives on a pirate ship. What can you see on his ship? (computer, chair, cat, pirate flag, pirate hat, cushion, bed, books, shelf)

- Do you like Red Ted's ship? What is wrong with it? (his ship is untidy) *Develop children's responses in relation to objects and place.*

- Where should the chair be? *Develop children's responses. Repeat this question replacing "chair" with the cat on the computer and the books on the floor.*

- If your bedroom looked like this, what do you think you would do? (tidy it up)

- When you tidy your room up, what do you do? (put things away in cupboards, etc.)

- Does anybody help you to tidy your room? (mum, dad, brother, sister)

- What do you think Red Ted should do? (tidy his ship) *Take suggestions as to where he might put some of the objects in the picture and why.*

- Explain that the computer can be used to move the objects in the picture.

Plenary

- If we wanted to change this picture on the Flipover Book what would we have to do? (cut it out).

- How did we move objects on the computer screen? (we had to click with the mouse to move them)

- What happened if you only clicked the mouse one time? (the picture just moved around the screen when you moved the mouse)

- What happened when you clicked again? (the picture stayed where you clicked)

- How did you get the cat where you wanted him then? (clicked on the cat, moved the mouse and then clicked again)

Labels and signs

Key Questions 2 ▼

Introduction

- What is Red Ted up to today? (he is sorting out one of his treasure chests)

- What has Red Ted got in his chest? (he has got a collection of labels and signs, some are in pairs, such as "Open" and "Closed")

- Does anyone recognise any of the signs and labels that Red Ted has? *Develop children's responses. If no response is given, select ones to discuss.*

- *Focus on particular labels/signs and the fact that the text comes in different sizes, colours and styles.* What does this mean? Why is it this shape? Why is the writing in this colour?

- What other labels/signs can you see in Red Ted's room? (there is a label on the door saying "Red Ted's room" and a sign which is his face, there is a label on his book, there are labels on his photographs)

- Look around the classroom, what labels and signs can you see? What do they tell you?

Plenary

- This week we have been looking at labels and signs. Who can tell me why we need labels and signs?

- What labels and signs did Red Ted have in his room. Why?

- *Point to the labels saying "Open" and "Closed". Where would you find these signs? Repeat for other pairs and individual ones.*

- Why is the text different sizes, colours and styles?

Red Ted finds treasure

Key Questions 3 ▼

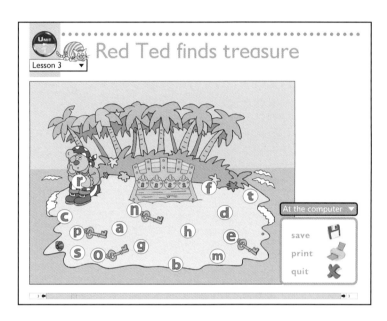

Introduction

- Red Ted has used his treasure map to help him. What has he found? (he has found a treasure chest on an island)

- What has Red Ted found around the treasure chest? What can you see? *The children should notice letters and keys.*

- Red Ted is holding a letter. What letter is it and why do you think he is holding it? (Red Ted is holding the letter "r", the first letter of his name)

- What letters can you see around the chest?

- I wonder why there were all these letters around the chest? *Develop children's responses.*

- *Write the letters on the board. Sound each one as you write.* Can anyone tell me a word beginning with "a"? *Work through some of the letters, taking more than one response for each letter.*

- Why do you think some of the letters have keys attached? (they open the locks)

Plenary

- Who can remind us about what Red Ted was doing in the picture?

- What did he find around the chest?

- Who was able to open the treasure chest?

- Can someone point to a letter on the picture and find that letter on the keyboard. *Repeat for a few letters, each time focusing upon the position of the letter, i.e. is it on the top, middle, bottom row, what letter is it next to etc.*

Red Ted wants a pet

Introduction

- Where do you think Red Ted is?

- What is he going to do?

- Who has got a pet at home? *Take a quick show of hands only at this stage.* Red Ted can't decide which pet to have. He can't make up his mind.

- *Discuss each pet separately.* Who has got a cat? Do you think Red Ted would like a cat? Why? *Repeat for other pets or a selection of pets.*

- Let's write the names of the animals on the board. Who can spell "cat"? *Do as a whole class or ask individual children. Write all the names of pets on the board to refer to later.*

- All of the animals Red Ted is looking at have three letters in their name. *Go through some again stressing the CVC pattern.*

Plenary

- Poor Red Ted. What couldn't he decide?

- What did we make on the computer for Red Ted to help him decide? *Show some of the printouts.*

- How did we make our list? What did we have to do? *Discuss entering words.*

- Was it easy or hard writing on the computer? *Discuss the children's responses – what was easy, what was hard.*

- Red Ted could have made a list. How else might he have made a list? (he could have written it)

- *Show the children a list made by Red Ted. It is not very easy to read. Compare this with the printout.*

- Which is easier to read? Why?

Red Ted plays a game

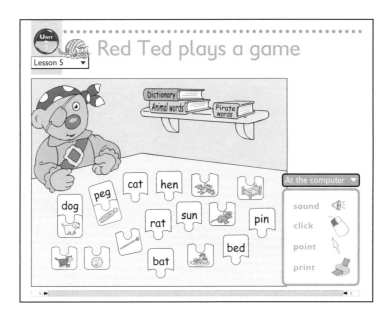

Introduction

- What is Red Ted doing in today's picture? (he is playing a game)

- What type of game is he playing? (he is doing a jigsaw)

- Who likes to play with jigsaws? What jigsaws do you have at home?

- Red Ted's jigsaw has words and pictures. How does Red Ted know which word goes with which picture? (he's matching the words to the pictures)

- *Point to one of the matched pictures and words.* Let's look at the ones he has already matched together. What is this a picture of? What does the word say? *Repeat, reinforcing that each word matches a picture.*

- Can we help Red Ted to match the rest?

- *Select a picture that is unmatched.* What is this a picture of? Can you find the word to go with the picture? *Ask a child to come and point to the correct word. Repeat for other unmatched pictures.*

Plenary

- Red Ted was playing a game. What game was he playing?

- What game did you play on the computer?

- How did the computer help you know which word to use? *Focus on the speech function.*

- Red Ted likes playing with words. On his shelf he has lots of books with words in them.

- *Point to the books as you discuss them.* There is a dictionary, a book of animal words and a book of pirate words.

- *Show the children a dictionary.* A dictionary is a word list. It is a list of words. If we need to spell a word we can look in here. A word list on the computer helps us write words we might not know how to spell.

Red Ted writes a letter

Introduction

- What can we see in the picture today? What is Red Ted doing? (he is writing a letter)

- *Read his unfinished letter including "I like to …". What does Red Ted like to do? (Red Ted likes to read) Children can use the picture and word clues in the thought bubbles.*

- Who is Red Ted writing to?

- Why is Red Ted writing a letter? (he is telling us about himself)

- Red Ted has some other letters. What letters has he received? (postcard, card, airmail letter) *Take one at a time and read.*

- Why do we write letters?

- This letter has a special envelope. *Show them the airmail sticker.* What do you think this means? (it comes from another country) *Explain the use of airmail.*

Plenary

- Red Ted is a very busy bear. He likes to write. What does he like to write? (letters and stories)

- In the picture there are other things he has written. Can you see some other things he has written? What are they? (a story, notes, calendar, shopping list)

- Which ones has he written on the computer?

- Is it better for Red Ted to write on the computer or by hand? (it depends on what he is doing)

- What have we written on the computer this week? *Read some examples of the letters.*

- How did the computer help us to write the letter?

What is the weather like?

Key Questions I ▼

Introduction

- Red Ted is on his ship. He can't decide what clothes to wear today. Can we tell what the weather will be like by looking at the picture? (yes, there are dark rain clouds, a rainbow and sunshine)

- What clothes do you think he should wear today? *Develop children's responses.*

- How could Red Ted find out what the weather is going to be like? (weather forecasts on the TV and radio, from the paper)

- Does anybody watch the weather forecasts on the television? What information do we get? (pictures, animation, writing, a presenter)

- *Show the children a map of the United Kingdom. Mark where Red Ted's ship might be. Show the children your weather pictures.* What pictures would you put on the map to show what the weather is like?

- *Show the children a weather map taken from a newspaper.* What will the weather be like? What weather pictures/symbols can you see?

- *Read the children some simple text to go with the weather map.* What might we say about our weather map? *If necessary model the presentation of information through role play.*

Plenary

- Red Ted needs some information about the weather. How could he get this information? (watch the TV, look at a paper, stand outside and look at the sky)

- Why do you think Red Ted wants to know what the weather is going to be like? (he doesn't know what to wear)

- Why do we need to know what the weather will be like tomorrow, next week? (in case we are going on holiday, having a birthday party in the garden or a sports day next week)

- Information about the weather is important. What other information is important to us? (times shops are open, time school starts, how much things cost, how to make a cake)

What can you hear?

Introduction

- Look at Red Ted. What do you think is the matter?

- What do you think he can hear?

- What is making Red Ted scared?

- What does the sound tell him? *Take each suggestion given by the children and elaborate.*

- What sort of noise would that be? *Take each sound and discuss whether it is a loud/soft noise.*

- Can you describe what the sound is like? (it is rumbling, crashing, wailing etc.)

- What else can you see in the picture that makes a sound?

- What does the sound tell Red Ted?

Plenary

- Do you remember why Red Ted was scared? (he heard noises that were frightening)

- If Red Ted was smiling, what might he have heard? What sound might make him happy? Why?

- Some sounds warn us of danger. Can you think of a sound that would warn us of something dangerous?

- What other sounds might Red Ted hear when he is on his ship?

UNIT 2

Treasure map

Introduction

- In the picture you can see Red Ted. What else can you see? (a map)

- What is a map? *Answers to this question and the following may depend upon work covered in the area of learning knowledge and understanding of the world (Foundation stage).*

- What does a map tell us? (how to get somewhere, what you can find there)

- *Point to each symbol separately.* What do these symbols mean on the map?

- So what does *this* map tell us? (how to get to the treasure) *If the children can't answer, prompt here by pointing at particular symbols.* What can you tell me about this island?

- *Read the written instructions Red Ted is holding.* What do these tell us?

- Red Ted has two different types of information. What are they? (pictures and written instructions)

Plenary

- Can anyone tell me, what is "information"?

- Red Ted had two different kinds of information. What did Red Ted want to know?

- How did Red Ted know where to go?

- How can information be shown? (in pictures, in words)

- Can anyone remember other types of information we have looked at this week? (books, passports, catalogues for example)

- How was this shown? What did it tell us?

Red Ted's holiday

Introduction

- Can anyone guess what Red Ted is doing today? (going on holiday)

- Are there any clues as to where he is going on holiday? (look at the contents of his suitcase)

- What information might we want to find out about Red Ted's holiday? (information such as what was the weather like, what did he eat, what did he do) *Encourage the children to pose questions.*

- Is there any information on the picture to tell us if Red Ted has been on holiday before? (stickers provide further information in a variety of forms such as flags, animals)

- Can you see Red Ted's passport? What does he need a passport for? *Children may have different experiences of passports – some may have their own. Discuss what information it holds and why we need passports.*

- *Point to the globe.* Does anyone know what this is?

- What is a globe? What are the blue areas? What are the green areas?

- What information does the globe tell us?

Plenary

- Who can tell me some information they have found out about Red Ted's holiday?

- Where is he going? (the seaside)

- What sort of weather will he find there? (stormy, windy, cold etc.)

- How do you know this? (children in coats, rough seas)

- What sort of clothes should Red Ted take? (warm clothes, coats)

Talking stories

Introduction

- What is Red Ted doing in today's picture?

- Red Ted likes to read. He likes to read a lot of different books. What types of books can you see on the table?

- What is a dictionary? Why would you use a dictionary? *Repeat these questions for the recipe book and the book on ships.*

- Who reads comics at home? What do you like about comics?

- Red Ted has a magazine. It is called "The Good Pirate". What do you think is inside the magazine?

- Can you think of any other types of books we read? (reading books, picture books, travel books)

Plenary

- Red Ted was reading some books. Can you remember the different types of books he likes to read?

- This week you have read a book. What was it called? What was it about?

- Who can tell me something that happened in the book?

- How was the story on the computer different to stories in books?

All about...

Introduction

- Red Ted is very busy today. Can anyone think what he might be doing? (he is making a display, finding information)

- What information can you see on his display? (information about treasure chests, what a pirate wears, what a pirate ship looks like, the name of a pirate)

- Look at the information. There are different types of information. What can you see? (photos, pictures, books, drawings, models)

- Red Ted is searching for more information. What is he using? (the computer) *Explain that he is searching on the Internet.*

- There is a tape recorder on the table. It says there is an interview with Pirate Jo on the tape. Does anyone know what an interview is? *Explain.*

- What do you think we might hear on the tape? *Develop children's responses.*

- Optional: play the tape of the interview and ask children about what they heard.

- Can you think of any other information Red Ted might include in his display?

Plenary

- Red Ted has been collecting information to make a display. Can you remember what was in his display?

- How is our display similar to Red Ted's? How is it different?

- Who can tell me one piece of information from our display?

- Who drew a picture for our display? Can you come and show me which one?

- Who typed a label for our display? What does the label say? Why did you make this label?

- Who recorded an interview? What was it about?

- If you met a pirate, what questions do you think you might ask? *Extend and elaborate children's responses.*

Where's Ted?

Introduction

- Where is Red Ted today? (he is on his pirate ship)

- What is Red Ted saying? Shall we read it together? (I have lost Little Ted. Can you find him?)

- Where do you think Little Ted might be hiding? *Look at the picture to see where he might be. Develop children's responses such as, inside the bed, under the bed, behind the cushion. Develop the children's use of positional language in their descriptions.*

- Do we know what Little Ted looks like? (there is a picture on the wall of Little Ted, he is small with orange fur and brown paws, he is wearing a blue jumper)

- Has anyone ever lost their teddy? How did you find it? Where was it?

Plenary

- What was the matter with Red Ted in the picture? (he had lost Little Ted)

- On the computer you had to find the two teddies. How did you do this? (used the mouse to control the pointer to move the objects around the screen)

- Where did you find the teddies? (behind the cupboard and under the cushion and bedspread)

- Some of you have hidden the teddies in the room again. *Get two or three children to stand up with their pictures.* Can you guess where the teddies might be in these pictures?

Jigsaws

Introduction

- What is Red Ted doing in the picture today? (he is doing a jigsaw)

- Why do you think he is scratching his head? (he doesn't know which piece to put in next)

- How could we help Red Ted finish the jigsaw? What information could we use to help us? (the completed picture and the pieces of the jigsaw, for example, straight sides mean outside pieces, the colours on the pieces show which part of the picture it is)

- What picture is he making? (a picture of himself)

- Which part of the picture has he already done? How can you tell? (he has finished the top side of the jigsaw because you can see his hat and his head)

- Red Ted has put out the four corners. Why has he done this do you think? (they are easy to find and can be used to show how big the jigsaw will be)

- What piece do you think he should use next? Look carefully at the picture he is making and the pieces on the floor (the side showing his flag).

- How could the computer make doing a jigsaw easy? (no small pieces to lose, easier to handle etc.)

Plenary

- Red Ted was making a jigsaw but he was stuck. You have all finished a jigsaw. How did you work out how to do it? *Encourage the children to think about the processes involved in sorting the pieces and the information from the picture and the pieces that helped them to complete it.*

- Can you tell Red Ted how to complete the jigsaw by giving him some information? *Get the children to describe the pieces carefully and to use correct positional language.*

- Who can give me some information about jigsaw number 2? How many pieces were in it? What is in the picture? Was it easier or harder than the first? Why? (more pieces) How did you work out how to do it? (used corner pieces, found straight edges, etc.)

What is it?

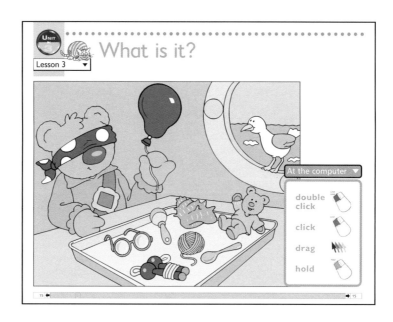

Introduction

- Red Ted is playing one of his favourite games. Can you guess what it is? (like a feely bag where you have to guess what the object is)

- What object is he holding? (a balloon)

- Do you think he will guess what it is? (yes, probably)

- Why? How would you know you were holding a balloon? *Develop children's responses. You could blindfold a child and get them to feel the balloon and describe how it feels.*

- *Point to one of the objects on the tray and develop children's responses.* Let's look at the other things on the tray. Who can give me one word to describe this? *Repeat with other objects.*

- Let's play a game with Red Ted. Look at these things and choose one on your own. Don't tell anyone which one you have chosen. Now think of a word or words you could use to help Red Ted find it on the tray.

If colour is chosen by a child, discuss how you cannot feel colour so that would not be a good word to use.

Plenary

- Red Ted has been playing a game. How did he find out what he was holding? (he used his paws to feel)

- When you were playing your game on the computer did you use your hands to feel the objects? (no, eyes)

- So we can use our hands and eyes to find out information. Can we use anything else? (we could use the other senses such as taste)

- Who used the tray to help with the game? How did it help you? (you could feel things to decide what was hard and what was soft)

- Who did the activity with the cars and bikes? How did you sort the objects? *Prompt for different criteria such as big and small, wheels/no wheels, colour, etc.*

Meet Mag Pie

Introduction

- This is one of Red Ted's friends. Her name is Mag Pie.

- What is Mag Pie up to in the picture? (she is tidying toys)

- What toys can you see? (balls and building blocks)

- Can you describe the toys? *The children might talk about colour, but prompt them to think about the size or shape of the objects.*

- Do you know the name for these shapes? (a sphere and a cube)

- How could Mag Pie tidy the toys? What could she do? *Encourage the children to talk about sorting the toys in different ways – by shape, by colour or by size.*

Plenary

- I have some labels here to put on the chests to help Mag Pie. *Put "spheres" or "balls" on one chest and "cubes" or "blocks" on the other.*

- Who can come and point to the toys that will go in this box? *Point to sphere/ball label and then the cube/block label.*

- *Repeat with labels for "small" and "big".*

- What other ways did you use to sort the toys on computer? Tell me more about the labels you would use.

- Does any one sort their toys at home? How do you sort them? *Talk about possibilities such as by colour, type of toy, etc. Prompt for other examples.*

Red Ted has lost his ship

Introduction

- Red Ted has a problem today. *Read through the title.*

- Has anyone ever lost anything? How did you find it? *Discuss what the children did in order to find the object they had lost for example, asked somebody, looked for the object.*

- If you asked somebody to help you find something you lost, what would you need to tell them? (what it is, what it looks like)

- Red Ted is trying to tell us about his ship. He is giving us information about his ship. What information is he giving us? *Use clues in thought bubbles. Go through what the ship is made from, the size of it, and how many masts, sails and windows it has.*

- Could we use this information to draw what Red Ted's ship might look like? *Ask children to come and draw aspects of the ship using the four clues on the Flipover Book page.*

- Is there anything else Red Ted could tell us to help him find his ship? *Discuss the children's answers and record these on the white board.*

- Look at the pictures of ships. Are any of these Red Ted's ship? Why not? *Go through each of Red Ted's "clues" and eliminate each of the ships, for example, the first found ship is too small.*

Plenary

- This week we have been thinking about information and key words. Who can tell me what information is? Why are key words important? (they make it easier to find and identify things)

- Red Ted gave us some information about his lost ship. What information did he give us? (how big the ship was, what it was made from, etc.)

- Did everybody manage to use the information on the computer to find the ship? What did Red Ted say about his ship?

- *Look at examples of the flag.* Who can give me some information about Red Ted's flag? *Write the key words on the board as they are spoken.*

Which is which?

Introduction

- What do you think Red Ted and Mag Pie are doing? Look at the picture for clues. (sorting treasure)

- *Point to different examples.* Look at the line of jewels. What can you tell me about the jewels? (they are big and small, different colours and shapes).

- Red Ted has some labels. Let's read them together. *Read all the labels together.*

- Mag Pie has matched some of the labels to some of the jewels. What labels has she put with the first jewel? Is she right?

- Are there any other labels she could put with the first jewel? What else could we try?

- How might we sort the second/third/ fourth/fifth jewel? What labels could we give them?

Plenary

- What do you think about Red Ted's sorting game? Was it hard or easy? Why?

- How did we play the game? What did we have to do?

- Can we help Mag Pie finish the game with my labels of key words? *Ask some children to come and add labels to the Flipover Book page.*

- Did anyone produce their own labels for the objects in the classroom? Tell me about them.

- What would happen if we changed the objects? (different labels might be required) *Ask for examples.*

Television studio

Key Questions 1 ▼

Introduction

- What can you see in the picture? (a news programme is being made, there are cameras, a control panel, a weather man, lights)

- What do you think the lady behind the desk might be saying? (telling the news – what has happened today around the world) *Ask the children if they know anything that has been in the news recently.*

- This man is going to talk about the weather. What do you think he might say about today's weather? Would the weather be the same all over the country?

- *Point to the camera operators.* What do these people do? *Talk to the children about the difference between live programmes like the news and recorded programmes, which are shown at a later time. Give examples of the children's favourite programmes to illustrate this.*

- *Discuss how the studio would be different if they were making, for example,* Blue Peter. (there would be more props, more things of interest to see)

Plenary

- Have you enjoyed playing in the TV studio?

- What did you use in your play and how did it help you? (cameras, tape recorders, etc.)

- *Point to the camera, laptop, weather forecaster's control button, control panel. Can anyone explain to me how this works and what it is used for?*

The weather forecast

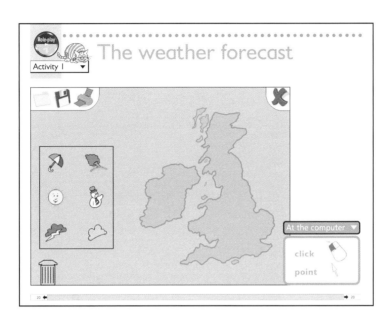

Introduction

- Do you watch the weather at home on your television?

- Why do we need weather forecasts? (severe weather warnings, whether to go on holiday, take an umbrella, know what clothes to wear)

- What do you think would happen if we didn't have weather forecasts?

- *Show the children one of your laminated weather symbols, cut out from Resource Sheet 11.* Look at this weather symbol. What does it mean? *Go through each of the weather symbols and ask the same questions.*

- *Place them on the map.* What can you tell me about the weather? *Repeat, moving the symbols around.*

- Would we use different symbols in the summer and winter? Why?

Interviewing people

Introduction

- What is happening in the picture? (a reporter is interviewing two people)

- What do you think the reporter is asking the father and child? *Develop responses from the children.*

- What sort of things might people want to ask questions about?

- Has anyone been stopped in the street and asked questions?

- How are they recording what the people are saying? (using a tape recorder and microphone)

- Is this a good place to interview someone? *Encourage the children to think here about noise levels in a busy street and hearing what people say.*

- What other places might you go to interview people? (shops, outside school or a cinema)

Using cameras

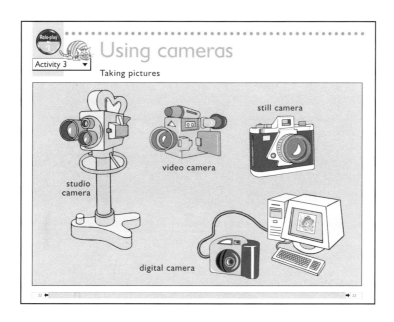

Introduction

- What can you see on our picture (four different types of camera)?

- Can you read the labels?

- Do you know how these cameras are different? What they are used for?

- *Point to each picture and discuss each type of camera. Clarify the difference between a digital and still camera. Show the children the real object when talking about a video recorder, digital camera and still camera.*

- *Discuss how each type of camera works by identifying key buttons and functions.*

- Who has got a camera at home? What pictures have you taken with your camera?

Star ship

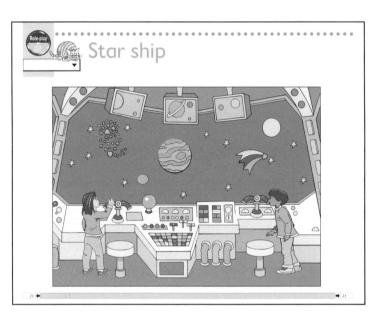

Introduction

- What can you see in the picture? (space, planet, stars)

- If we were looking out of this window where would we be? (on a rocket, in space, in a star ship)

- Who can read the words at the top here? (star ship)

- What is a star ship? (a rocket, a spacecraft)

- Are star ships real?

- Who can tell me anything about space and flying in space? *Develop the children's responses. Make notes on a whiteboard for reference later.*

- Who would/would not like to go up in space? Why? Has anybody seen any programmes on television about space? What happens?

- *Point to Mars.* Do you think there is anything living on this planet? What might it look like?

- Can you see anything on the picture that would help us control/fly/navigate this star ship? *Discuss the control panel.*

Plenary

- Who liked working on the star ship? Why?

- We have used a computer and other things in this role-play. What different things have we done? *Recap on each of activities, what technology was used and for what purpose.*

- *Show one of the crew member's ID cards.* How did we make these ID cards? What did we do?

- How did we use the computer to make an alien face? Could we have done this activity away from the computer? (yes, using pencil and paper) Was it easier or harder on computer? Why?

- What did we learn when using *Granada Colours*? *Focus on the tools used and what they helped to do.*

- What did we need to think about when using the alien toy and the space grid on the computer? (direction and turns) What happened when you followed the instructions? (the star ship crashed)

- Who managed to get the star ship to Mars? Was this easy or hard? Why?

To the planet

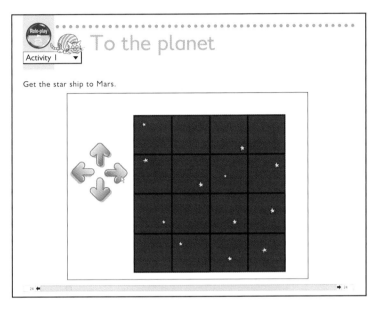

Introduction

- What can you see in the picture? (space, stars, black, grid, arrows)

- What do you think the arrows are for? Think about our work moving the alien. (the arrows control movement)

- *Show the picture of the star ship prepared from Resource Sheet 30. What is this? Repeat with the other pictures, then place each one on the grid starting with the star ship in the bottom left and Mars in the top right corner.*

- If we want to get the star ship to Mars which direction do you think we need to move? You cannot move diagonally. *Highlight on the grid what diagonally means.*

- What is the shortest journey? *Use laminated arrow cards from Resource Sheet 29 to record different journeys.*

- Can anyone see a different journey that takes the star ship to Mars?

- What would happen if I placed the comet here on the grid? What would our journey look like now? *Emphasise the point that the star ship would need to avoid the comet.*

- *Repeat several times adding further pictures when appropriate. Record each journey using the arrow cards.* Now we are going to try this activity on the computer.

Teacher's Support

CREATING A SET OF FOLDERS

It is important in terms of classroom management that you have disk space in which your class can save their work. It is therefore recommended that you make a set of personal folders for your class. Not only will this give the children a consistent location in which to store and find their work, but it will also allow you to check completed work if you don't have a printout.

This is the recommended pathway to use in creating your folders:
My Computer/My Documents/Year R_P1/Child's name.

My Computer and **My Documents** are folders that already exist on your hard drive.

To create a Year R_P1 folder follow these instructions:
1. Double click on **My Computer**.
2. Double click on **My Documents.**
3. When the **My Documents** window is open, go to **File** and **New**.
4. Select **Folder** from the top of the menu.
5. A new folder appears in the **My Documents** window with the name "New Folder" highlighted.
6. Type in "Year R_P1". The computer will over-type automatically.

You now have a master folder for your Year R/P1 class work.

You can store all of the children's work in this folder by creating a new personal folder for each child.

Double click on the **Year R_Y1** folder you have just created.

When the window is open, use the same process to create new folders and name one for each child in your class. Create one for yourself at the same time and a general folder that you can use for shared work.

The children can now save work directly into their personal folders. Instruct them to use the initials of their name + the file name. (Using their full name will make the file name too long to handle.)

If you have chosen to network *Granada Toolkit* and *Nelson Thornes Primary ICT*, it is likely you will want

pupils to save their files to the network, rather than the hard drive of each machine. If you do not already have a suitable space on your network for pupils to save their files to, one will need to be created. Your network administrator should be able to provide an appropriate solution for your network.

ORGANISING YOUR FOLDERS

Windows provides a basic filing structure for you with ready-made folders such as **My Documents**. You can customise this structure by adding your own folders, or even adding folders inside folders (subfolders).

Move or copy a folder into another folder

1. Open the window containing the folder to be moved or copied.
2. Open the destination folder.
3. Select the folder to be moved or copied.
4. To move the folder, drag it and drop it in the destination folder window. To copy the folder, hold down the Ctrl key while dragging.

Rename a folder

1. Click the folder to select it.
2. Click the folder name (not the folder icon).
3. Highlight the name and, with the name selected, type a new name, or click to position the insertion point and then edit the name.
4. Press Enter.

Delete a folder

1. Open the drive or folder containing the folder to be deleted.
2. Select the folder.
3. Press the Delete key.
4. Click **Yes** to delete the folder or file and send it to the Recycle Bin.

If you are deleting a folder that contains files, click the appropriate button if Windows asks you to confirm before deleting some types of files.

Move a file into a subfolder

1. Open the window containing the file and the subfolder.

2. Select the file to be moved.

3. Drag the file and drop it on top of the subfolder.

Move a file into another folder

1. Open the window containing the file to be moved.
2. Open the destination folder.
3. Select the file to be moved.
4. Drag the file to the destination folder and drop it on to a blank spot.

Copy a file into a folder

1. Open the window containing the file to be copied.
2. Open the destination folder.
3. Select the file to be copied.
4. Hold down the Ctrl key, drag the file to the destination folder, and drop the file's copy on a blank spot.

Move or copy several files

1. Select a file to be moved or copied. Hold down the shift key and click on any other files you want to move or copy.
2. Hold down the Ctrl key if the files are to be copied, and then drag the files and drop them at the new location.

TEACHING THE CHILDREN TO SAVE WORK

When you introduce the idea of saving to a personal folder, explain that the computer contains a lot of empty folders and that these folders are a bit like boxes. Tell the children that you have created a large box that you have named **Year R_P1** and that you have put smaller boxes inside the large Year R_P1 box for them save their work in; one named after each child in the class.

Save and Save As …

The first time that you save a document, you should do so using the **Save As…** option from the **File** menu. This is because the first time that you want to save something you need to tell the computer the name that you want to save it with and the location into which you want to save it. If you have chosen to network the Pupil CD-ROM, using **Save As…** will also ensure that the original document on your network is not overwritten.

If you have set up your folders in the suggested location, they will choose Drive C:/My Documents/Year R_P1/child's name. Thereafter, if you make a change to that saved document, you can simply click on the save icon in the menu bar or choose **Save** from the **File** menu. The computer will then save any changes that you have made using the same name and location. Alternatively, simply hold down the **Ctrl** key and press **S** on your keyboard, as a shortcut to save. With Reception/P1 children, you will, at least initially, have to save for the children in most cases.

Storing information on a floppy disk

To save work on a floppy disk you simply use the Save As... procedure and select the $3\frac{1}{2}$ Floppy (A:) from the **Save in**: box.

ACTIVITY DATA FILES

Many of the data files in Reception/P1 are activity data files that do not require any additional software to be accessed. These are mostly click and point activities designed to familiarise the children with control of the mouse and moving items around the screen.

THE ICONS

Many of the activity data files include a simple tool bar with various icons along the top of the screen. It would be useful to familiarise the children with the functions of each of the icons, although an audio prompt and a short animation have been added to help the children to remember. The icons are as follows:

 Open a previously saved version of the data file

 Allows the child to save the data file in her/his "My documents" folder (see "Creating a set of folders" on page 94).

 Print a data file

 Quit or exit the program.

Please note that opening and saving require the children to locate their folders – they are likely to require careful support with this.

Customising *Granada Toolkit* screens

You can customise the toolbars in *Granada Writer* and *Granada Colours* by adding and removing items, and enabling or disabling certain functions. Customised versions can be named and saved for future use, giving you the facility to offer the software across a range of abilities. It is even possible to configure the software to the needs of individual children.

Please note, however, that when working with data files you will need to customise each computer **after** the data file has been opened.

Click on the small icon in the very top left-hand corner of the screen and choose Customise from the menu to launch the set up manager.

Now, simply tick or clear the options you require. As you do this you will see the changes take immediate effect. Select one of the slots marked "empty" from the "Name" drop-down list, and then click the **Admin** button and replace "empty" with a name of your choice.

A customised setting would be very useful for Reception/P1 children. You might wish, for example, to include large icons and include only those that will be used in the lesson, to remove the word bank or clip art bank when not in use or set a larger or more "infant friendly" font such as Sassoon Infant.

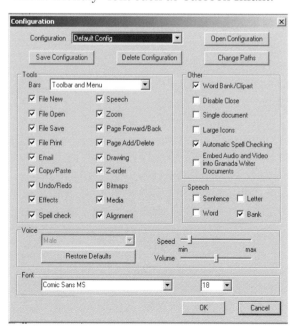

To save a configuration so that it can be used again, select an "empty" slot for the name. If you do not select an "empty" slot the changes you make will only apply to the current session. Click **Save Configuration** to confirm your choices. If you would like to edit the default configuration of *Granada Writer*, choose the setting called "Default" instead of an empty slot.

Granada Writer in the classroom

Granada Writer is a versatile talking word processor and desktop publisher package. Unlike word processing packages aimed at the adult market, you can click anywhere on the page and start typing. There are also many other facilties that make *Granada Writer* an ideal tool for the classroom, including a word bank, picture bank and a comprehensive speech facility, all of which can be added to and adapted by the teacher.

The various media banks are not used in Reception/P1 activities, though the concept of word lists is introduced, as some data files on the Reception/P1 Teacher's and Pupil CD-ROMs include prepared word lists embedded within the files. The word lists allow Reception/P1 children who can read simple cvc words but not yet spell them, to produce a simple story or sentence. The lists obviously have a more limited vocabulary than the *Granada Writer* word banks, which they will begin to use in Year 1/P2. However, if you wish your children to start using the word banks, you can make your own focused word banks by following the instructions in the *Granada Toolkit* user manual. In this way you can supply focused lists of words that are currently being used in other lessons or are relevant to the topic on which you are currently working.

Sound and video clips have also been embedded within data files supplied on the Teacher's and Pupil CD-ROMs (in lessons 2 and 4 in Unit 2), though again you might direct some of your more confident children to use the prepared *Granada Writer* sound and video clip banks.

Like any other word processor, *Granada Writer* offers children experiences in two main areas. Firstly, it is a composition tool that allows them to manipulate words in ways that are quite impossible on paper.

Secondly, it offers them opportunities to present work in exciting and interesting ways. (A very positive thing for children who find presentation difficult.)

As well as supporting virtually all PC sound and image formats, the package also supports Web pages – a feature of growing importance in the current environment.

THE "SAY" FACILITY

A particularly useful feature of the *Granada Writer* package is its "Say" facility. This facility enables children to type or select text and hear it spoken by the computer. It provides extra support for many learners and is a valuable tool in helping children to gain confidence in assembling their text independently.

A number of settings exist that enable you to hear individual words, sentences, paragraphs or even a whole page.
- To hear a word from your page you simply highlight that word and click on the "Say" icon (a speech bubble) in the toolbar at the top of the screen.
- To hear a word from the word bank you simply highlight that word within the bank by left clicking on it and then right click to hear the word spoken.

With the "Say" facility enabled, *Granada Writer* can speak back to users. Highlighting a word and clicking the "Say" icon will make *Granada Writer* speak it. It will also speak sentences back too.

Granada Writer uses the sentence terminators – full stops, question marks, exclamation marks – to delimit sentences. When it recognises a sentence terminator it will automatically speak the sentence back.

The "Say" facility can be customised using the Setup Manager. The options allow you to speak each letter, word or sentence as it is being typed. If you prefer, however, the sound facilities can be switched off altogether. For instructions on how to get to the customising screen see pages 96.

CREATING A LABEL TEMPLATE
(Unit I Lesson 2)

It is a good idea to have a label template prepared as the children will be too young to change the font size themselves. Go to the customise option (see page 96 for details) and change the font size. The options listed only go up to 72 but you can type in a higher size than this. 150 produces an appropriate size if used with lanscape printing. You can create a text box for the label, using the **Add Rectangle** option in the **Tools** menu.

To change printing to landscape, choose the **Page Setup** option from the **File** menu. Click on the landscape icon.

Save this file (if you have followed the instructions on page 94 for organising files you can save it to your general folder) for the children to use for their labels.

CARD KEYBOARDS AND PLAY KEYBOARDS
(Unit I)

Children will gain a lot from "playing" with keyboards not attached to a computer as this will help develop their confidence in using a real keyboard. It helps develop familiarity with the position of particular keys, allows them to get a feel for typing, and will give them greater opportunity to "play" writing on a computer. Old keyboards from non-functioning computers should be kept, or collected for this purpose. Also keyboard images can be downloaded from the Internet and then printed, stuck onto card and laminated.

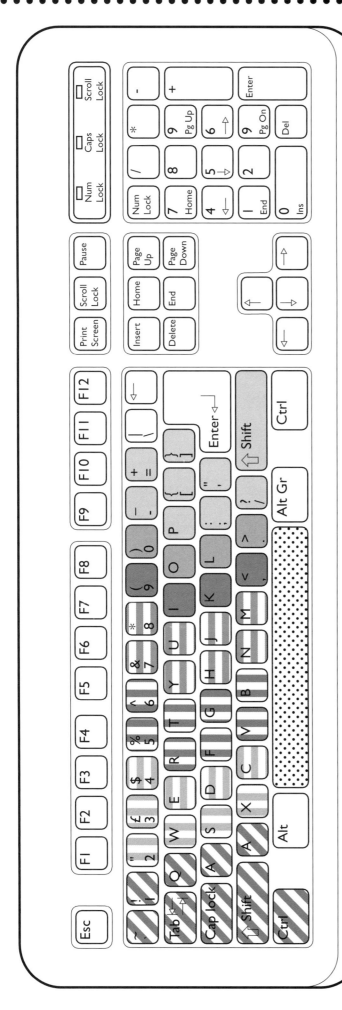
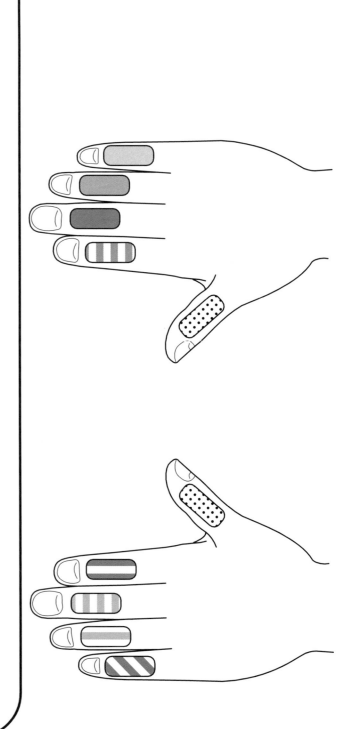

98

TEACHING TYPING TO VERY YOUNG CHILDREN
(Unit I)

When learning to write the children need to develop good habits in holding a pencil and forming letters. The same applies to using a computer keyboard. The children need to learn good habits from the moment they start typing, using the individual keys to make letters. If poor habits are picked up then the children will either need to relearn skills or continue as inefficient writers. This obviously takes time and practice is important which is why it is desirable to have alternative keyboards for the children to use when access to the computer is limited. Where and when possible try to reinforce the use of all fingers and give the children simple exercises to practise using several fingers to write easy words, such as the "cat", "sat", "rat" group using the left hand or "pin", "pot", "pit" using the right hand. The chart on page 98 shows the correct fingers for each key.

You can purchase software from The Learning Company, who provide activities and games to teach young children basic keyboard skills.

DEVELOPING PICTURE PROCESSING
(Units 2 and 4)

Picture processing can be seen as a natural progression from using the computer to process words. As the children learn to manipulate text, so they learn to manipulate images, providing the same dynamic approach to editing and alteration that word processing does with writing. Underpinning this approach is the concept of providing individual children with an alternative to the constraints and restrictions that are offered by traditional classroom materials and modes of working. In exploring new horizons, the children need to develop a range of concepts, skills and knowledge that is commensurate with their age and maturity. With the range of graphics software available today, a developmental approach is both desirable and possible.

Ideally, with any painting/image editing software that you use with the children, try to divide their experience into three parts. Firstly, "give them a taste": demonstrate how certain essential things are achieved with the hardware and software provided (being careful to leave some aspects open for discovery). Secondly, allow the children time to play and experiment with the facilities on offer. When they have "discovered" an interesting technique they will quite often be motivated to attempt an ambitious picture or design. Thirdly, give them time to develop and amend their "work of art" (perhaps at lunch times or in sessions before/after school). This time is amply rewarded by the tremendous pride and satisfaction gained – especially when a well-executed piece of work is printed and appears on a wall display.

INTRODUCING YOUNG CHILDREN TO GRAPHICS
(Units 2 and 4)

Children today are much better equipped to deal with the human-computer interface thanks to icons, working windows and particularly to the mouse. However, just watch any child trying to manipulate the mouse and you will begin to realise one major difficulty! The problem essentially is that the mouse is just too big for little hands.

Several companies have stepped in with "mini" mice that offer a better solution than the full-sized mouse. SEMERC's Mini Mouse is designed for small hands. This small, translucent mouse functions just like a standard mouse. However, it illuminates when clicked to confirm the press (USB version only). Both teacher and the child can see if a successful press has been made.

GRANADA COLOURS

Granada Colours is a painting and image-editing program that enables the children to draw and paint pictures, or to edit existing images quickly and easily. It contains a number of very useful features and these, coupled with its ease of use, make *Granada Colours* the ideal tool for children at all levels. The software is fully configurable, thus teachers can set up the software to match the abilities of their class or the required learning outcome of a particular lesson. Tools can be added and removed from the toolbars, and a choice of colour palettes give differing levels of complexity (see below). For example, teachers working with young children or those with learning difficulties will find the option to increase the size of the tools or icons particularly useful.

You start *Granada Colours* from the Launcher program, or by going to the Windows Start menu and selecting *Granada Colours* from the Granada Learning folder.

Customising *Granada Colours* to suit your needs

(See instructions on pages 96 on Customising Granada Toolkit screens.)

Colours

The colour palette is displayed to the right of the work area. When the cursor is over the colour palette it turns into a dropper tool which can be used to select colours. When the dropper is over the colour palette another box will appear above the active colour box; this new box will display the colour the dropper is resting on. To make this colour the active colour, click with the left mouse button.

You can customise the palette from the General Properties screen (see Customising *Granada Toolkit* screens on page 96).

The Bank

The Bank is used to access the shapes and tools that you will need to make a picture. There are four separate tool bars in The Bank, two of which you will use in Reception/P1.

Resting the mouse pointer on an icon will bring up a description of it. Right clicking on the icon will bring up a further menu of options.

At Reception/P1 level you will mainly be using the shapes and the floodfill tool. Allow the children to practice or "play" with these tools as much as time allows.

The Shapes

You access the shapes through the Shapes toolbar. At this level it is recommended that you restrict the children's use to the Outline Square, Outline Circle, Outline Polygon and Outline Star. One click starts the shape and a second fixes it.

The Floodfill Tool

The floodfill tool "floods" a selected area with the selected colour. Conversely using the tool outside a selection will change the colour of the background work area. Using traditional methods you might be able to apply just one colour to an object or area picture. In *Granada Colours* you are able to experiment as many times as you want.

Some children may be ready to use the following tools:

The Pen Tools

The pen tools give the choice of drawing in freehand or with straight lines. A single click begins the operation, a second fixes it. Children (and teachers) may take some time to familiarise themselves with this technique.

The Freehand Brush

This brush acts in the same way as a paintbrush in the hand. It creates a thick freehand brush stroke in the chosen colour.

The Spray Gun

The spray gun tool applies a paint spray effect to the work area. This is a very effective tool for showing texture in pictures, for example clouds, hair, the leafy parts of trees or the effects of light at night.

TALKING BOOKS
(Unit 2, Lesson 5)

Electronic talking books serve two main purposes:
- they introduce the children to the key ICT idea that computers can use text, pictures and sounds to convey information (or multimedia)
- they are invaluable teaching resources for literacy/language lessons, as they can be used in the same ways as "big books" for shared reading or for supported reading practice alone. They can also be used for word and sentence level work.

The best "talking books" include simple navigation, a good combination of text, pictures and sounds, a fair amount of visual impact and, of course, an interesting and well presented story. In addition, the children should be able to interact with the text and quickly familiarise themselves with "talking book" conventions such as back and forward arrows. *Nelson Thornes Primary ICT Reception/P1 Teacher's* and *Pupil*

CD-ROMs include a very simple "talking story", in which Red Ted loses his hat.

For more information about electronic "talking books", including some recommendations, visit the Literacy Time web site at
http://www.becta.org.uk/literacy.html

SORTING AND MATHEMATICAL DEVELOPMENT
(Unit 3)

"Mathematical development depends on becoming confident and competent in learning and using key skills," (QCA, 2000, p 68). One of these key skills is sorting. Sorting is the prerequisite for handling data and requires the children to observe, describe and compare objects looking for similarities and differences. Sorting leads the children:

*   to make choices and decisions in mathematics (shall we sort into big and little or into circles and not circles?)
*   to use information (I know this is a circle so it must go in this box)
*   to learn new mathematical vocabulary
*   to begin to explain mathematically (it can't be a circle because it has got straight sides)
*   begin to reason mathematically (its not as big as this shape so it can't go in this set).

ROLE PLAY
(Unit 4)

(Detailed notes on the use and purposes of role-play and ICT can be found in the introduction on page v.)

DIGITAL CAMERAS
(Unit 4, Television Studio role play)

Digital cameras are becoming more commonplace in schools and offer versatility and opportunities to be creative in using ICT. You can see the images quickly, getting immediate feedback to decide whether the picture is clear, focused, centred and includes all necessary parts. Images can easily be erased and a new image taken. Editing the composition develops skills in decision-making, critical reflection and fitness for purpose – does the picture give you the information you wanted? Digital cameras allow children to develop and refine camera skills by trial and error, by taking images again and again until it is right. The unwanted images can be erased easily reducing wastage and cost. The digital camera can also help the children to focus in on an activity to explore at a later date. Much of the role-play process is lost once the activity has been completed. Using the camera allows the children to review what happened and to develop a greater awareness of the processes by referring to the photographs in future activities. In the role-play units the children could also use digital cameras to take portraits of each other.

Children in Reception/P1 will need adult guidance and support in using a digital camera. Skills such as looking through the viewfinder, holding the camera steady and standing at an appropriate distance from the object apply to both still and digital cameras and need to be taught. Taking a good digital image is no different from taking a picture with an optical 35mm camera, and the same rules for good picture-taking apply. The difference is that there is no film, the images being stored in the camera's memory. Make sure the child wears the safety wrist strap to reduce the risk of dropping and breaking the camera. The latest digital cameras are very user friendly. Look for an auto-setting model as these automatically focus the images.

Down loading digital images

If possible ask the ICT subject leader at your school to take you step-by-step through the procedure for downloading the images from the camera to the computer as each piece of software works in different ways.

The children can see the pictures they have taken on the LCD colour screen immediately, so they can monitor the results of each shot. Once transferred to the computer, the images can be sharpened a little, dropped into a DTP document, given a caption and printed out directly on the colour printer.

A computer with a fast memory is ideal for processing and editing the images taken so that the process is not time-consuming and therefore frustrating for the children who are eager to see the results of their efforts.

The software provided permits images to be viewed as thumbnails which resemble slides. Selecting all or some of the thumbnails and dragging the selection onto a directory on the hard disk downloads the full images and saves them. The exceptions to this are Sony Mavica cameras, whose images are stored in the form of JPEGs (compressed images) and saved directly onto floppy disks, which is very convenient for school use and compatible with Mac Power PCs as well as PC computers.

PROGRAMMABLE TOYS
(Unit 4 Role-play 2)

Robot vehicles like Roamer (Valiant Technology) and Pixie (Swallow Systems) provide a foundation of concepts on the road to understanding programming and computer control. Each one operates independently of the classroom computer and, being battery operated, has no leads and plugs. Robot vehicles teach a great deal about feedback and sensing: those essential principles of computer control! The instructions that follow are based on the Roamer.

Roamer

A Roamer resembles a small flying saucer and offers a platform on which young children can create Roamer characters by adding mechanical components and/or reclaimable materials. Roamer is programmed via a control panel on its back. It travels in pre-set "Roamer-lengths". Instructions, based on Logo commands, are entered via a touch keypad comprising move, turn, wait, repeat, procedure and sense keys. Up to 60 commands can be entered allowing Roamer to perform many hundreds of operations as both procedures and repeats can be used. The capacity to use procedures permits a top-down approach to programming. To keep things simple, use of variables or recursion are denied. Units of distance and turning can be scaled as necessary to suit the abilities of the children. The optional Roamer Control Pack offers lights, sensors and motors connected with via a small control interface which screws on underneath the robot and transforms a Roamer into a control device. Try making a Roamer sheep dog which responds to whistles by changing direction. Children love it! Valiant Technology offer a range of other enhancements including identity kits, a

pen pack, and Roamer World that enables Roamer programs to be downloaded to a PC for storage or further editing.

BASIC COMMANDS FOR THE ROAMER

Below is the instruction pad for the Roamer.

You must press "**CM**" twice to clear the memory first before you give instructions.

To move the Roamer forward or back:
- Press **CM** twice.
- Simply press one of the direction arrows and then the number of steps you want the Roamer to move, followed by **GO**.
- For example, (forward arrow) 4 would move the Roamer 4 steps forward.

To move the Roamer a specified angle to the left or right:
- Press **CM** twice.
- Press the left or right arrow.
- Then type in 90 (for right angle).
- Press **GO**.

The Roamer will turn to the left or right the angle you have specified.

In Reception/P1 it is likely that you will have to do much of this programming yourself, especially moving left or right.

One of the aspects of using a Roamer that many teachers overlook is care of the batteries. Without fully functioning batteries, a floor robot is virtually useless. If they are not handled correctly, the batteries are likely to become unreliable and cease to function.

HOW TO CHARGE THE BATTERIES

a) Ensure the power adapter jack plug is disconnected from the charger socket.

b) Insert the two Lead Acid batteries into the charger housing, ensuring the spring contacts align correctly with the metal strips in the charger. Remember you must charge both batteries otherwise the charger won't work.

c) Connect the power adapter jack plug into the charger socket. The red lamp above the charger socket should illuminate; then plug in the power adapter to the mains electricity supply and switch on.

d) The red lamp should stay illuminated, indicating fast charge. It will remain lit until the batteries are fully charged. Should your batteries already be fully charged, the lamp will extinguish after a few seconds.

Should the lamp go out instantly, the batteries are not charging because they have failed. You must purchase replacements from your Valiant supplier.

e) When the batteries are fully charged (after about 10 hours) you should switch of the mains electricity supply and disconnect the jack plug from the charger before removing the batteries.

BATTERY CARE AND WHEN TO CHARGE THE BATTERIES

a) You MUST charge the batteries immediately on receipt, they may have been in storage for some time and will require charging to ensure they become fully charged before initial use.

b) You should recharge the batteries immediately AFTER each use. This is the only way of ensuring they are not unintentionally discharged.

c) If you intend to store your batteries you must first charge them; they will then need recharging at least once every 6 months afterwards.

NEVER leave batteries in the Roamer during holidays or other extended periods. NEVER leave batteries in the charger when it is not recharging. In either case, the batteries will discharge.

Links between Reception *Nelson Thornes Primary ICT* and the National Curriculum Programmes of Study

Working towards Level 1

Unit 1: Words and pictures

	1a	1b	1c	2a	2b	2c	2d	3a	3b	4a	4b	4c	5a	5b	5c
Lesson 1		●	●			●				●	●				
Lesson 2		●												●	
Lesson 3		●	●											●	
Lesson 4		●	●											●	●
Lesson 5		●	●	●											
Lesson 6		●	●		●	●									

Unit 2: Presenting information

	1a	1b	1c	2a	2b	2c	2d	3a	3b	4a	4b	4c	5a	5b	5c
Lesson 1		●	●			●	●	●	●						●
Lesson 2	●	●	●					●						●	
Lesson 3	●	●	●					●						●	
Lesson 4	●	●	●	●						●	●	●		●	
Lesson 5	●	●	●	●			●							●	
Lesson 6		●	●					●	●	●	●	●		●	

Unit 3: Sorting information

	1a	1b	1c	2a	2b	2c	2d	3a	3b	4a	4b	4c	5a	5b	5c
Lesson 1		●	●			●				●	●				
Lesson 2		●	●	●	●	●				●	●				
Lesson 3		●	●	●	●										●
Lesson 4		●	●	●	●					●	●				
Lesson 5		●	●	●	●										
Lesson 6		●	●	●	●					●	●				

Unit 4: Role play*

	1a	1b	1c	2a	2b	2c	2d	3a	3b	4a	4b	4c	5a	5b	5c	5d
Role play 1	●	●	●	●				●	●	●			●	●	●	
Role play 2		●	●			●	●	●	●				●	●		

*Also turn to page 106 for links between Unit 4 and *Curriculum Guidance for the Foundation Stage* (DfES/QCA, 2000)

All Units/lessons include links to other key aspects of the *Curriculum Guidance for the Foundation stage* – see 'Integrated tasks and links' section in Unit Overviews.

Links between P1 *Nelson Thornes Primary ICT* and the 5–14 National Curriculum and the 5–14 National Guidelines

Working towards Level A

Strand: Using the technology

Attainment targets	Unit/lesson
Use a mouse to point and click	U1/L1, U2/L1, L3 & L4, U3/L1-L4, U4/RP1-RP2
Start up/shut down the computer	*
Use a keyboard/concept keyboard	U1/L2–L6, U3/L6, U4/RP1
Print by clicking 'print' button	*
Save and retrieve work with support	*

Strand: Creating and presenting

Attainment targets	Unit/lesson
text Create, enter and amend one or more sentences without teacher support	U1/L6, U4/RP1–RP2
graphics Create a picture using simple software	U2/L6, U4/RP2
multimedia Add text to a picture	U1/L3–L5, U4/RP1

Strand: Collecting and analysing

Attainment targets	Unit/lesson
Use non-computer database	U3/L1–L6
Use simple predefined computer databases	U3/L1–L6

Strand: Searching and researching

Attainment targets	Unit/lesson
Recognise that information is available electronically	U2/L1–L6, U4/RP1

Strand: Searching and researching

Attainment targets	Unit/lesson
Recognise that information is available electronically	U2/L1–L6, U4/RP1

Strand: Communicating and collaborating

Attainment targets	Unit/lesson
Show awareness that messages can be communicated electronically	U4/RP1–RP2
Give simple comparisons with telephone/post	–

Strand: Controlling and modelling

Attainment targets	Unit/lesson
Follow directional instructions	U2/L5, U4/RP2

* Links exist through all levels of the scheme

Links between Reception *Nelson Thornes Primary ICT* and Curriculum Guidance for the Foundation Stage

Unit 4: Role Play 1 – TV studio

Early Learning Goals	1	2	3	4	5	6	7	8	9	10	11	12	13	14	15	16	17	18	19	20
CLL	✔	✔			✔	✔	✔	✔											✔	
PSE	✔	✔		✔				✔												
MD																				
KUW					✔															
PD	✔						✔	✔												
CD	✔	✔	✔		✔															

Unit 4: Role Play 2 – Space: star ship

Early Learning Goals	1	2	3	4	5	6	7	8	9	10	11	12	13	14	15	16	17	18	19	20
CLL	✔	✔	✔	✔	✔	✔	✔	✔			✔	✔						✔	✔	
PSE	✔	✔		✔	✔		✔	✔		✔		✔								
MD		✔	✔	✔		✔	✔						✔							
KUW	✔	✔		✔			✔		✔											
PD	✔						✔	✔												
CD	✔		✔	✔	✔															

Links between P1 *Nelson Thornes Primary ICT* and Curriculum Framework for children 3 to 5

Unit 4: Role Play 1 – TV studio

Key aspects*	1	2	3	4	5	6	7	8	9	10	11	12	13	14	15	16	17	18	19	20
EPS	✔							✔	✔											
CL	✔									✔	✔		✔			✔				
KUW	✔		✔				✔													
EAD	✔		✔	✔			✔													
PDM	✔					✔		✔												

Unit 4: Role Play 2 – Space: star ship

Key aspects*	1	2	3	4	5	6	7	8	9	10	11	12	13	14	15	16	17	18	19	20
EPS				✔	✔	✔			✔											
CL				✔			✔	✔	✔	✔		✔		✔		✔	✔			
KUW			✔				✔		✔					✔	✔	✔	✔	✔		
EAD	✔	✔	✔	✔	✔															
PDM		✔			✔	✔														

(* The numbers along the row relate to the features of learning described within each key aspect, e.g. Emotional, Personal and Social Development 1 is 'develop confidence, self-esteem and a sense of security')

KEY		
	CLL = Curriculum, Language and Literacy	CD = Creative Development
	PSE = Personal, Social and Emotional Development	EPS = Emotional, Personal and Social Development
	MD = Mathematical Development	CL = Communication and Language
	KUW = Knowledge and Understanding of the World	EAD = Expression and Aesthetic Development
	PD = Physical Development	PDM = Physical Development and Movement

Equipment list

The following equipment is required for Reception/P1 of this course:

Hardware requirements

A multimedia PC (minimum 32MB RAM, Windows 95) including speakers
High colour graphics 800 × 600 resolution
Quad speed CD-ROM drive
A colour printer

Software requirements

Granada Toolkit (Granada Learning) containing each of the following:
● A word processing/DTP package with speech facility that allows children to match words and pictures and contains word, picture and sound banks
● Paint and object-based drawing software

Nelson Thornes Primary ICT Resources CD-ROMs
Nelson Thornes Primary ICT Work Card CD-ROM (for printing out additional copies of the Work Cards)

Other requirements

A blackboard and chalk or flip chart and marker

A teddy bear

A3 size card keyboard or play keyboard

Jigsaws

Picture dictionaries

Video of weather forecasts

Map of the UK with weather symbols

Tape recorder and blank tapes

Holiday brochures and postcards

Camera (digital or still)

Video recorder and tapes

Variety of different types of books

Pre-recorded tape of interview with pirate

A globe

A passport

Collection of interesting objects (see Unit 3)

Collection of balls and blocks

Enlarged laminated pictures of 50p and 5p coins

Examples of wood and metal

A toy ship with a mast

Glossary

a: drive
the name given to the drive for *floppy disks*

Animation
a *simulation* of movement by displaying a series of pictures, or frames, in fast succession

Bitmap image
an image created from tiny coloured squares (pixels) on the computer screen

c: drive
the name given to the computer's *hard disk drive*

card keyboard
a play keyboard to familiarise children with the location of keys

CD-ROM (Compact Disk Read-Only Memory)
a disk used for storing electronic information. Can store up to 450 *floppy disks* worth of information

Clip art
illustrations stored on the computer that can be inserted into a *document*

Cursor
a small arrow or flashing line that indicates where you are on the computer screen. Also known as a *pointer*

Data
a distinct piece of information. This can exist in a variety of forms

Digital camera
a camera that records images in a digital form allowing easy transfer to a computer where the images can be altered, stored or viewed

Disk drive
a machine that reads *data* from and writes data onto a disk

Document
a file created with a *word processor*. Can contain text, images, sounds and other objects

File
data that has been entered and saved on the computer with a name

Floppy disk
a removable disk that the computer uses to store information

Folder
a collection of computer *files*

Font
the style of typeface used

Graphics
the creation, editing and printing of pictures. Computer graphics are stored using two main methods: *vector* graphics (stored as a list of vectors) and *raster* or *bitmap* graphics (stored as a collection of dots or pixels)

Hard disk
a magnetic disk used to store *data*. Permanently connected to the computer as part of the *hardware*

Hard disk drive
a *disk drive* that reads from and writes to a *hard disk*; the computer's permanent data store

Hardware
the physical machinery and equipment that makes up a computer

Icon
a small picture on the computer screen that represents a command or function

Import
to bring *data* (such as a picture or text) from one *file* into another

Media
different means by which information is communicated (e.g. the medium of sound; the medium of video)

Megabyte (MB)
a unit used to measure computer memory

Modem
a device which uses telephone lines to connect computers to each other for sending communications

Mouse
a hand-held device that controls the movement of the *cursor* on the computer screen

Multimedia
communication that uses any combination of different *media*. In computing, the presentation of text, *graphics*, video, *animation* and sound in an integrated way

Navigate
to find your way around *software* or the *World Wide Web* by following links

Network
a group of interconnected computers that communicate with each other and share resources such as printers and *software*

PC
a personal computer

Pictogram
a pictorial representation of statistics on a chart or graph

Picture bank
a bank of images grouped according to particular themes

Pointer
see *cursor*

Program
an organised list of instructions
that causes the computer to behave
in a predetermined way

RAM (Random Access Memory)
the working memory of the
computer. Used for storing *data*
temporarily while working on it.
Can be accessed directly and
immediately, in contrast to other
media such as a magnetic tape
which must be wound to a certain
point to retrieve data. RAM is
known as volatile memory; it will
disappear if the power is switched
off before it is saved to disk

Raster image
a *bitmap image*

ROM (Read-Only Memory)
memory that can be read but not
changed and is used to store the
essential *software* of the computer.
ROM is known as non-volatile
storage; its content is kept even if
the power is switched off

Simulation
the imitation of a real
phenomenon

Software
programs that tell the computer
what to do

Stamp
a small prepared *graphic* which
can be "stamped" as a repeated
image onto the screen

Sound bank
a bank of sounds grouped
according to particular themes

Talking book
a book displayed on the computer
screen, accompanied by a speech
facility to read out the text. Usually
contains animation

Text box
a frame around a piece of text
which allows the text to be
manipulated

Toolbar
a bar that runs horizontally or
vertically across the screen
containing icons that represent the
commands that can be used in the
open *program*

Vector image
a way of producing pictures
whereby the image is saved as a
file containing the instructions for
how to draw it from a set of
coordinates. Unlike bitmap images
they can be easily resized without
loss of quality

Video bank
a bank of video clips grouped
according to particular themes

Window
a division of the computer screen
that has boundaries and is usually
rectangular in shape

Word bank
a bank of words grouped
according to particular themes

Word processor
1. A *program* used to create and
print (chiefly textual) documents
that might otherwise be prepared
on a typewriter
2. A computer which is designed
specifically for word processing

World Wide Web
a collection of *Internet* sites. It is
called a Web because all of the
individual sites are linked together
and users can travel from one site
to another by clicking on different
links